GOODSON MUMBA

Public Administration

Theory, Policy, and Practice for Modern Governance

First edition

ISBN: 9798334060999

This book was professionally typeset on Reedsy.
Find out more at reedsy.com

Contents

Preface

Public administration stands at the intersection of governance, policy, and management, serving as the backbone of governmental operations and societal development. It is an ever-evolving field that demands a deep understanding of theory, practical application, and the intricate dynamics between public institutions and the citizens they serve. This book, "Public Administration: Theory, Policy, and Practice for Modern Governance," is designed to provide a comprehensive exploration of the fundamental principles, contemporary challenges, and future directions in public administration.

The genesis of this book lies in the recognition of the crucial role that effective public administration plays in shaping societies, driving progress, and addressing the multifaceted challenges of the 21st century. From ensuring equitable service delivery and fostering social equity to navigating crises and leveraging digital advancements, public administrators are at the forefront of creating resilient, inclusive, and responsive governance systems.

The structure of this book reflects a deliberate effort to blend theoretical foundations with practical insights, offering readers a holistic perspective on public administration. Each chapter delves into core concepts, presents contemporary debates, and highlights real-world applications, making it a valuable resource for students, scholars, practitioners, and anyone interested in the workings of public administration.

Key Features of the Book:

1. **Comprehensive Coverage:** The book spans a wide range of topics, from the historical evolution of public administration and key theoretical frameworks to modern challenges such as digital governance, social equity, and crisis management.
2. **Practical Insights:** Case studies, real-world examples, and best practices are integrated throughout the chapters, providing readers with practical insights into the application of public administration principles in diverse contexts.
3. **Current Trends and Future Directions:** Special emphasis is placed on emerging trends, innovative practices, and the future trajectory of public administration, equipping readers with the knowledge to navigate and shape the evolving landscape of governance.
4. **Interdisciplinary Approach:** Recognizing the interconnectedness of various fields, the book adopts an interdisciplinary approach, drawing on insights from political science, economics, sociology, and management to enrich the understanding of public administration.
5. **Engaging and Accessible:** The content is presented in an engaging and accessible manner, with clear explanations, illustrative examples, and thought-provoking questions designed to stimulate critical thinking and discussion.

This book is the culmination of extensive research, collaboration, and a shared commitment to advancing the field of public administration. I am deeply grateful to the many scholars, practitioners, and students whose insights, experiences, and feedback have shaped the content of this book. Their contributions have been invaluable in ensuring that this work is both academically rigorous and practically relevant.

As you embark on this journey through the pages of "Public Administration: Theory, Policy, and Practice for Modern Governance," I hope you find inspiration, knowledge, and a renewed sense of purpose in the vital work of public administration. Whether you are a student beginning your studies, a scholar seeking deeper insights, or a practitioner navigating the complexities of governance, this book is intended to serve as a trusted companion and a source of guidance in your endeavors.

Thank you for joining me in this exploration of public administration. Together, let us strive to create more effective, equitable, and resilient governance systems that serve the needs of all citizens and contribute to the well-being of our global society.

Sincerely,

Goodson Mumba

Acknowledgement

I would like to eternally and gratefully acknowledge the Almighty God for the infinite intelligence from His universal mind where we draw from all that we come to know and are yet to know. May I also acknowledge and thank everyone that has played a part in my journey of life in terms of spiritual, moral, emotional and material support.

Dedication

I extend my sincerest gratitude to my beloved wife, Edith Mumba, and our children, Angelina, Lubuto, Letticia, Lulumbi, and Butusho, for their unwavering support and understanding throughout the conception, writing, and eventual publication of this book, despite the sacrifices and challenges they endured.

Disclaimer

This book is a work of fiction. Names, characters, businesses, places, events, and incidents are either the products of the author's imagination or used in a fictitious manner. Any resemblance to actual persons, living or dead, or actual events is purely coincidental.

1

Chapter 1: Introduction to Public Administration

Definition and Scope of Public Administration

D r. Robert Hayes stood at the podium in the large lecture hall, the early morning sunlight casting a warm glow over the rows of attentive students. This was the first day of his course, "Foundations of Public Administration," and he was eager to set the tone for the semester. He knew that understanding the basics of public administration was crucial for his students, many of whom would become future leaders in government and public service.

Dr. Hayes began by introducing himself and then launched into the first topic: the definition and scope of public administration. He explained that public administration is essentially the implementation of government policies and the management of public programs. It involves organizing public resources, managing public affairs, and delivering services to the public. He emphasized that it's the vital link between political decisions and the citizens those decisions impact.

One student, a young woman in the front row, asked why it was so important to start with definitions rather than jumping straight into practical aspects. Dr. Hayes smiled and explained that understanding the definition and scope of public administration is like understanding the rules and objectives of a game before playing it. Without this foundational knowledge, it would be impossible to effectively analyze, improve, or innovate within the field.

As he continued, Dr. Hayes highlighted the various activities encompassed by public administration, including policy formulation, budgeting, human resources, and ethics. He noted that public administration operates at all levels of government—local, state, national, and even international—and isn't limited to government entities but also includes non-profits, NGOs, and private sector collaborations.

When another student asked about the historical evolution of public administration, Dr. Hayes provided a brief overview. He traced its origins from early monarchies focused on taxation and law enforcement, through the complexities introduced by the Industrial Revolution, to the sophisticated administrative structures of modern times. He mentioned key milestones, such as the creation of modern civil services in the 19th century and the introduction of New Public Management in the late 20th century.

A third student raised his hand and asked about the differences between public and private administration. Dr. Hayes explained that while both share many techniques, their purposes and accountabilities differ fundamentally. Private administration aims for profit maximization and shareholder value, whereas public administration prioritizes public welfare, equity, and transparency. He added that the public sector operates under greater scrutiny and accountability to the citizens.

Another student then inquired about the role of public administration in modern governance. Dr. Hayes responded by saying that public administration is indispensable. It is the mechanism through which policies are translated into actionable programs, ensuring that resources are allocated efficiently, services are delivered effectively, and public interests are safeguarded. In today's world, with challenges such as climate change, social inequity, and rapid technological advancements, public administration is the linchpin that holds governance together.

Dr. Hayes concluded his lecture by previewing the topics they would explore in future classes, such as current trends and future challenges in public administration. He assured the students that they would delve deeply into the historical context, current practices, and future directions of the field. He encouraged them to think about how they could contribute to a more effective, ethical, and equitable public service.

The students left the lecture hall buzzing with excitement, eager to learn more. Dr. Hayes watched them go, satisfied that he had laid a strong foundation for the semester ahead.

Historical Evolution of Public Administration

Dr. Robert Hayes stood at the front of the lecture hall, the same warm sunlight illuminating the eager faces of his students. With the first lecture behind them, the students were already deeply engaged, ready to delve further into the rich tapestry of public administration.

"Today," Dr. Hayes began, "we're going to explore the historical evolution of public administration. Understanding its past helps us appreciate the complexities and advancements of the present, and guides us in shaping its future."

He clicked to a new slide, revealing a timeline marked with key historical milestones. As he spoke, the students listened intently, the air thick with anticipation.

"Public administration has ancient roots," Dr. Hayes explained. "It dates back to early civilizations like Mesopotamia and Egypt, where rulers organized large-scale irrigation projects and managed vast empires. These early forms of administration were primarily about control and resource management."

He paused, letting the weight of this ancient heritage sink in. One student, a young man named Alex, raised his hand and asked how these early practices influenced modern public administration.

Dr. Hayes nodded appreciatively. "Great question, Alex. These early efforts laid the groundwork for administrative systems by introducing concepts like bureaucracy and centralized control. However, it wasn't until much later that public administration began to take on a more structured form."

He moved the timeline forward, stopping at the Han Dynasty in China. "During the Han Dynasty, we see the emergence of a merit-based civil service, a significant advancement. Officials were selected based on examinations, an early precursor to the modern idea of recruiting based on qualifications."

A hand shot up from a student named Maria, who asked about similar developments in other parts of the world.

"Indeed, Maria," Dr. Hayes replied, "similar advancements

were happening elsewhere. For example, in the Roman Empire, administrative techniques were refined to manage its vast territories. The Romans developed a sophisticated legal system and administrative practices that influenced European governance for centuries."

He clicked to the next slide, featuring images of medieval Europe. "During the Middle Ages, public administration took a backseat to feudal systems. However, the Renaissance and the Enlightenment brought renewed interest in organized governance. Thinkers like Machiavelli and Hobbes began to theorize about statecraft and the role of public administrators."

As he spoke, the students scribbled notes furiously, captivated by the evolution of their field. Dr. Hayes then shifted to the 19th century, a pivotal era in the history of public administration.

"The Industrial Revolution," he said, "was a game-changer. With rapid urbanization and industrialization, the need for efficient public administration became apparent. It was during this period that we saw the birth of modern civil services, starting with the British Northcote-Trevelyan Report of 1854, which advocated for a professional, merit-based civil service."

A student named Jamal asked how these changes spread globally.

"Good question, Jamal. The principles established in Britain quickly influenced other nations. For example, the Pendleton Civil Service Reform Act of 1883 in the United States marked the beginning of professional public administration in America. This era also saw the emergence of public administration as an academic discipline, with scholars like Woodrow Wilson advocating for its study and professionalization."

He clicked to a final slide, highlighting the 20th century. "In the 20th century, public administration continued to evolve. The New Deal in the United States, the rise of welfare states in Europe, and the decolonization movements around the world all demanded more sophisticated administrative structures. This period also saw the development of new theories, such as New Public Management in the late 20th century, which sought to make public administration more efficient by borrowing techniques from the private sector."

Dr. Hayes wrapped up the lecture by emphasizing the importance of this historical context. "By understanding where we come from, we can better navigate where we are and envision where we need to go. Public administration is a dynamic field, constantly evolving to meet the needs of society."

The lecture ended with students deep in thought, their notebooks filled with notes. Dr. Hayes felt a sense of accomplishment, knowing that he had not only informed his students but also inspired them. As they left the hall, discussing the day's lesson among themselves, Dr. Hayes began preparing for the next topic, eager to continue this intellectual journey with his enthusiastic students.

Key Theories and Concepts

Dr. Robert Hayes looked out over his class, pleased to see the students still buzzing with energy from their discussion on the historical evolution of public administration. Today, he would guide them through the key theories and concepts that have shaped the field. He knew this lecture was crucial for laying a theoretical foundation that would support their understanding of more practical applications.

"Good morning, everyone," Dr. Hayes began, adjusting his glasses. "Today, we're diving into the key theories and concepts that form the backbone of public administration."

He clicked to the first slide, which displayed the title: "Classical Theories."

"Let's start with classical theories," he said. "These theories were developed during the early 20th century and laid the groundwork for modern public administration. Frederick Taylor's Scientific Management, for example, emphasized efficiency and productivity through the scientific study of work methods."

A student named Rachel raised her hand. "Wasn't Taylor's approach criticized for being too mechanical and dehumanizing?"

"Absolutely, Rachel," Dr. Hayes responded. "While Taylor's methods significantly improved efficiency, they often ignored the human aspect of work. This led to criticisms and the development of more human-centered theories."

He clicked to the next slide, which highlighted Henri Fayol's Administrative Theory. "Fayol, on the other hand, focused on the functions of management—planning, organizing, commanding, coordinating, and controlling. His principles of management, such as unity of command and division of work, are still relevant today."

Another student, Kevin, asked how these theories influenced public administration specifically.

"Great question, Kevin. Both Taylor and Fayol's theories contributed to the development of bureaucratic structures in public administration, emphasizing clear hierarchies and specialized roles."

Dr. Hayes then introduced Max Weber's Bureaucratic Theory. "Weber's theory of bureaucracy is one of the most influential in public administration. He argued that a rational-legal authority structure, characterized by clear rules, impersonality, and merit-based advancement, is the most efficient way to organize large-scale organizations."

He noted that Weber's model provided a framework for the development of modern public bureaucracies, which prioritize efficiency, predictability, and rule-based governance.

Next, Dr. Hayes transitioned to the Human Relations Movement, clicking to a slide featuring Elton Mayo and the Hawthorne Studies. "Mayo's work marked a shift from mechanical views of management to an understanding of the social dynamics of organizations. The Hawthorne Studies revealed that social factors and worker satisfaction significantly impact productivity."

A hand went up from a student named Sarah, who asked about the implications of these findings.

"Mayo's findings highlighted the importance of considering workers' needs and motivations," Dr. Hayes explained. "This led to the development of more participatory and employee-centered management approaches in public administration."

Moving on, he introduced Herbert Simon's Decision-Making Theory. "Simon challenged the classical theories by emphasizing the importance of decision-making processes. He introduced the concept of 'bounded rationality,' which recognizes the limitations of human decision-makers and the need for satisficing—seeking satisfactory rather than optimal solutions."

As Dr. Hayes continued, he highlighted Douglas Mc-

Gregor's Theory X and Theory Y. "McGregor's theories offered contrasting views of worker motivation. Theory X assumes that employees are inherently lazy and need to be closely supervised, while Theory Y posits that employees are self-motivated and thrive on responsibility. These theories have profound implications for management styles in public administration."

A student named Brian asked which theory was more applicable in the public sector.

"Both theories have their place," Dr. Hayes replied. "However, modern public administration tends to lean towards Theory Y, promoting empowerment and participatory management to foster innovation and motivation among public servants."

Dr. Hayes concluded with New Public Management (NPM), clicking to a final slide that read: "New Public Management and Governance."

"NPM emerged in the late 20th century, advocating for the adoption of private sector practices to improve public sector efficiency. It emphasizes results-oriented management, competition, and customer service. While controversial, NPM has led to significant reforms in many countries."

He ended the lecture by summarizing the importance of these theories. "Understanding these key theories and concepts is crucial for anyone in public administration. They provide the intellectual tools to analyze, design, and manage public organizations effectively."

The students were clearly intrigued, their notebooks filled with notes and questions. Dr. Hayes felt a sense of satisfaction, knowing he had provided them with a strong theoretical foundation. As the students filed out, discussing the various theories, he began preparing for the next lecture, eager to continue their exploration of public administration.

Public vs. Private Administration

Dr. Robert Hayes glanced at his watch, noting it was time to begin another lecture. The students had settled into their seats, ready for the day's discussion on the differences between public and private administration. This was a topic that often sparked lively debates, and he was eager to see their reactions.

"Good morning, everyone," Dr. Hayes greeted. "Today, we're going to explore the distinctions between public and private administration. Understanding these differences is essential for navigating the complexities of governance and management."

He clicked to the first slide, which featured a comparison chart titled "Public vs. Private Administration."

"Let's start with the basics," Dr. Hayes began. "Public administration refers to the management of governmental operations, while private administration involves the management of private sector enterprises. Although both aim to achieve efficiency and effectiveness, their objectives, accountability, and operational contexts differ significantly."

He noted the first key difference: **Objectives and Goals.**

"In public administration, the primary goal is to serve the public interest and promote the common good," Dr. Hayes explained. "This means providing services like education, healthcare, and public safety, which are essential for societal well-being. Conversely, private administration focuses on profit maximization and shareholder value."

A student named Emily raised her hand. "So, does that

mean public administration is more ethical because it serves the public interest?"

Dr. Hayes smiled at the insightful question. "Not necessarily, Emily. Both sectors face ethical challenges, but their ethical frameworks differ. Public administrators are guided by principles of transparency, equity, and accountability to the public. Private administrators are driven by market competition and customer satisfaction. Both can be ethical, but the nature of their accountability varies."

He moved on to the next slide, highlighting **Accountability.**

"In public administration, accountability is to the public and elected officials," he said. "Public administrators must adhere to laws, regulations, and public scrutiny. This can sometimes slow down decision-making processes but ensures transparency and public trust. In contrast, private administration is accountable to owners, shareholders, and customers, which often allows for quicker decision-making but can lead to less transparency."

A hand went up from Jason, a student in the middle row. "What about efficiency? Isn't the private sector generally more efficient?"

"That's a common perception, Jason," Dr. Hayes acknowledged. "Private organizations often have more flexibility to innovate and streamline operations, which can lead to greater efficiency. However, public administration deals with more complex and often contradictory demands, such as balancing efficiency with equity and ensuring public access to essential services."

Dr. Hayes clicked to another slide labeled **Decision-Making Processes.**

"In the private sector, decision-making is typically centralized and driven by market demands," he explained. "Decisions can be made swiftly to adapt to market changes. In public administration, decision-making involves multiple stakeholders, including elected officials, interest groups, and citizens. This can be more time-consuming but ensures that diverse perspectives are considered."

A student named Priya asked how this impacts the implementation of policies.

"Excellent point, Priya," Dr. Hayes said. "The inclusive decision-making process in public administration can make policy implementation slower but often results in more comprehensive and equitable outcomes. In contrast, the private sector can implement changes quickly, but these might not always account for broader social impacts."

He then discussed **Resource Management.**

"Public administration deals with public resources and must ensure their fair distribution," he noted. "This includes managing budgets, human resources, and public assets with an emphasis on accountability and equity. Private administration, on the other hand, focuses on optimizing resource use to achieve business goals, often with a greater emphasis on cost-efficiency and innovation."

Finally, Dr. Hayes addressed **Performance Metrics.**

"Performance in public administration is measured by service quality, equity, and public satisfaction," he said. "Public administrators must balance various competing interests and goals. Private administration measures performance primarily through financial metrics like profitability and market share."

A student named Brian asked about the impact of these differences on employee motivation.

"Good question, Brian," Dr. Hayes replied. "In the private sector, financial incentives and career advancement often drive employee motivation. In the public sector, motivation is frequently linked to public service values and the desire to make a positive impact on society. Both sectors face challenges in maintaining employee motivation, but the sources of motivation can differ significantly."

As he wrapped up the lecture, Dr. Hayes summarized the main points. "Understanding these differences is crucial for anyone pursuing a career in public administration. Both sectors have their strengths and challenges, and recognizing these can help you navigate and succeed in whichever path you choose."

The students left the lecture hall deep in thought, discussing the complexities of public and private administration. Dr. Hayes felt satisfied, knowing he had sparked critical thinking and provided valuable insights. As he prepared for the next lecture, he looked forward to continuing this journey of discovery with his students.

Role of Public Administration in Modern Governance

The lecture hall was buzzing with anticipation. Dr. Robert Hayes had promised an engaging discussion on the role of public administration in modern governance, a topic he believed was crucial for understanding the field's real-world impact. He knew this lecture would connect the theoretical foundations with practical implications, inspiring his students to appreciate the profound influence of public administration on their daily lives.

"Good morning, everyone," Dr. Hayes began, as the room quieted down. "Today, we'll explore the pivotal role public administration plays in modern governance. This is where theory meets practice and where your future careers can make a significant difference."

He clicked to the first slide, which read: "Public Administration: The Backbone of Governance."

"Public administration is the backbone of governance," Dr. Hayes said. "It ensures that policies made by elected officials are effectively implemented and that public services are delivered efficiently and equitably."

He noted the first key role: **Policy Implementation.**

"Public administrators are responsible for translating policy decisions into actionable programs and services," he explained. "Without effective public administration, even the best policies would fail to reach the people they're intended to help. Think of public health initiatives, education reforms, and infrastructure projects—public administrators make these possible."

A student named Jessica raised her hand. "Can you give us an example of how public administration impacts policy implementation?"

Dr. Hayes smiled. "Certainly, Jessica. Consider the Affordable Care Act in the United States. The law itself is a policy decision made by legislators, but its success depends on public administrators. They design the systems for enrolling people, manage the databases, ensure compliance, and provide customer service. Without their work, the policy would remain just words on paper."

He moved to the next slide: **Public Service Delivery.**

"Public administration ensures that essential services like

healthcare, education, transportation, and public safety are available to all citizens," he continued. "These services are fundamental to the quality of life and the functioning of society. Public administrators manage these services, ensuring they are accessible, efficient, and responsive to the public's needs."

A student named Marcus asked about the challenges faced in delivering public services.

"Good question, Marcus," Dr. Hayes responded. "Challenges include limited resources, bureaucratic inefficiencies, and changing public needs. Public administrators must be adept at problem-solving, resource management, and adapting to new technologies and methods."

The next slide highlighted **Regulation and Enforcement.**

"Public administrators also play a crucial role in regulation and enforcement," Dr. Hayes explained. "They develop and enforce regulations that protect public health, safety, and welfare. This includes everything from environmental regulations to consumer protections and workplace safety standards."

Sarah, a student from the middle row, raised her hand. "How do public administrators balance regulation with economic growth?"

"Excellent question, Sarah," Dr. Hayes said. "It's a delicate balance. Public administrators must ensure regulations protect the public without stifling innovation and economic growth. This often involves stakeholder engagement, impact assessments, and continuous review of regulations to keep them relevant and effective."

He then discussed **Crisis Management.**

"Public administration is vital in managing crises," Dr.

Hayes continued. "During natural disasters, public health emergencies, or other crises, public administrators coordinate response efforts, mobilize resources, and communicate with the public. Effective crisis management can save lives and restore normalcy."

A hand went up from a student named Alex. "Can you give an example of a successful crisis management effort?"

"Certainly, Alex," Dr. Hayes replied. "Consider the response to Hurricane Katrina. While the initial response faced criticism, subsequent improvements in emergency management led to a more effective response to Hurricane Sandy. Lessons learned from past failures helped public administrators develop better coordination, resource allocation, and communication strategies."

The next slide was titled **Promoting Social Equity.**

"Public administration plays a key role in promoting social equity," Dr. Hayes said. "This involves ensuring that public policies and services are fair and inclusive, addressing disparities, and working towards social justice. Public administrators advocate for marginalized communities, develop inclusive policies, and ensure equitable access to services."

Priya, a student known for her insightful questions, asked, "What are some strategies public administrators use to promote social equity?"

"Good question, Priya," Dr. Hayes said. "Strategies include conducting equity assessments, engaging with diverse communities, developing targeted programs for underserved populations, and continuously evaluating outcomes to ensure equity goals are met."

He concluded with **Enhancing Citizen Engagement.**

"Finally, public administration enhances citizen engagement," Dr. Hayes explained. "This means involving citizens in decision-making processes, increasing transparency, and fostering trust in government. Public administrators create platforms for citizen input, ensure open communication, and use technology to engage with the public."

The students were visibly engaged, their faces reflecting deep thought and understanding. Dr. Hayes wrapped up the lecture, emphasizing the importance of their future roles.

"Remember," he said, "as future public administrators, you will be at the forefront of implementing policies, delivering services, managing crises, promoting equity, and engaging citizens. Your work will directly impact the lives of people and the functioning of society. Embrace this responsibility and strive to make a positive difference."

As the students left the lecture hall, their conversations buzzed with excitement about the potential impact they could have in public administration. Dr. Hayes watched them go, feeling proud of the seeds of inspiration he had sown. He looked forward to the next lecture, where they would continue their journey into the intricate world of public administration.

Current Trends and Future Challenges

Dr. Robert Hayes walked into the lecture hall, a palpable sense of excitement in the air. His students had been enthusiastic throughout the course, and he was eager to discuss the final subpoint of their first chapter: the current trends and future challenges in public administration. This lecture would bridge their foundational knowledge with the evolving landscape they would soon navigate.

"Good morning, everyone," Dr. Hayes began, the hum of

student chatter fading into attentive silence. "Today, we'll wrap up our introduction by examining the current trends shaping public administration and the future challenges you'll likely face in your careers."

He clicked to the first slide, which read: "Digital Transformation and E-Government."

"One of the most significant trends is digital transformation," Dr. Hayes explained. "E-Government initiatives aim to improve public services and citizen engagement through technology. This includes online portals for services, digital communication platforms, and data-driven decision-making."

A student named Lisa raised her hand. "How has digital transformation impacted public administration so far?"

Dr. Hayes smiled. "Great question, Lisa. Digital transformation has streamlined processes, reduced costs, and increased accessibility. For instance, filing taxes, applying for permits, or accessing public records can now be done online, making services more efficient and user-friendly. However, it also presents challenges such as cybersecurity risks and the digital divide."

He clicked to the next slide: "Emphasis on Sustainability."

"Another trend is the growing emphasis on sustainability and environmental governance," Dr. Hayes continued. "Public administrators are increasingly tasked with developing and implementing policies that promote sustainable development, reduce carbon footprints, and address climate change."

A student named Mark asked, "What are some examples of sustainable policies?"

"Good question, Mark," Dr. Hayes responded. "Examples include renewable energy initiatives, waste reduction programs, sustainable urban planning, and policies promoting green transportation. Public administrators must balance economic growth with environmental protection, a complex but crucial task."

The next slide was titled "Focus on Social Equity and Inclusion."

"Public administration is also focusing more on social equity and inclusion," he said. "This involves addressing systemic inequalities, ensuring fair distribution of resources, and creating inclusive policies that consider diverse populations."

Priya, always quick with insightful questions, raised her hand. "What strategies are used to promote social equity?"

"Excellent question, Priya," Dr. Hayes replied. "Strategies include community engagement, targeted programs for underserved populations, equity assessments, and inclusive policy design. Public administrators work to ensure that everyone has access to essential services and opportunities, regardless of their background."

He moved to the next slide: "Collaborative Governance."

"Collaborative governance is another emerging trend," Dr. Hayes explained. "This involves multiple stakeholders, including government agencies, private sector partners, and non-profit organizations, working together to address complex issues. This approach leverages diverse expertise and resources for more effective solutions."

Alex, a student from the front row, asked, "Can you give an example of collaborative governance in action?"

"Certainly, Alex," Dr. Hayes said. "An example would be public-private partnerships in infrastructure projects. Governments collaborate with private companies to fund, build, and maintain public infrastructure like roads, bridges, and public transport systems. This collaboration can bring innovation and efficiency but also requires careful management to ensure public interests are protected."

He clicked to the next slide: "Resilience and Crisis Management."

"Given the increasing frequency and severity of natural disasters, pandemics, and other crises, resilience and crisis management have become critical," Dr. Hayes continued. "Public administrators must develop strategies to prepare for, respond to, and recover from crises."

Jessica raised her hand. "How do public administrators build resilience?"

"Good question, Jessica," Dr. Hayes replied. "Building resilience involves comprehensive risk assessments, robust emergency response plans, inter-agency coordination, community engagement, and continuous training. It also requires investing in infrastructure that can withstand disasters and ensuring that recovery plans are in place."

Finally, he addressed "Globalization and Interconnectedness."

"The final trend we'll discuss is globalization and the increasing interconnectedness of our world," he said. "Public administration now operates in a global context, dealing with transnational issues like migration, trade, and climate change. This requires collaboration across borders and understanding international regulations and standards."

Brian, a student from the middle row, asked, "What are the challenges of globalization for public administration?"

"Excellent question, Brian," Dr. Hayes said. "Challenges include managing international relations, navigating different legal and regulatory frameworks, and addressing global issues that require coordinated responses. Public administrators must be adaptable and culturally aware to effectively manage these complexities."

As Dr. Hayes wrapped up the lecture, he summarized the main points. "Understanding these current trends and future challenges is crucial as you prepare to enter the field of public administration. You'll need to be adaptable, innovative, and collaborative to address the evolving needs of society and ensure effective governance."

The students left the lecture hall deep in thought, discussing the various trends and challenges. Dr. Hayes felt a sense of accomplishment, knowing he had provided them with a comprehensive overview of the dynamic field they were about to enter. He looked forward to guiding them through the rest of the course, eager to see how they would apply this knowledge in their future careers.

$$2$$

Chapter 2: Theoretical Foundations of Public Administration

Classical Theories of Administration

D r. Robert Hayes stood at the front of the lecture hall, the anticipation of a new topic sparking curiosity among his students. Today's lesson would delve into the classical theories of administration, laying the groundwork for their understanding of the field's theoretical foundations.

"Good morning, class," Dr. Hayes greeted, his voice carrying a tone of enthusiasm. "Today, we embark on a journey through the classical theories of administration, which laid the groundwork for modern public administration as we know it."

He clicked to the first slide, displaying the title: "Classical Theories."

"Our exploration begins with the early 20th century thinkers who laid the groundwork for our understanding of administration," Dr. Hayes continued. "These theorists sought to bring scientific principles to the management of organizations, revolutionizing the way we think about governance and bureaucracy."

He paused, allowing the weight of their impending discussion to settle over the room.

"Our first stop on this journey is Frederick Taylor's Scientific Management," Dr. Hayes announced, clicking to a slide featuring Taylor's stern visage.

"Taylor's approach emphasized efficiency and productivity through the scientific study of work methods," he explained. "He believed that by breaking down tasks into their smallest components and standardizing processes, organizations could achieve maximum efficiency."

As Dr. Hayes spoke, the students scribbled notes furiously, captivated by the historical significance of Taylor's work.

"However," Dr. Hayes continued, "Taylor's theories were not without controversy. Critics argued that his methods led to dehumanization in the workplace, reducing workers to mere cogs in a machine."

A hand shot up from a student named Emily. "How did Taylor's theories impact the field of public administration?"

"Great question, Emily," Dr. Hayes replied. "Taylor's ideas had a profound influence on public administration, particularly in the realm of bureaucracy. His principles of scientific management were adopted by government agencies seeking to streamline operations and improve efficiency."

He clicked to the next slide, featuring Henri Fayol's Administrative Theory.

"Fayol, a French mining engineer, introduced a more holistic approach to management," Dr. Hayes explained. "He identified five functions of management—planning, organizing, commanding, coordinating, and controlling—and fourteen principles of management, which emphasized unity of command, division of work, and equity."

The students nodded along, recognizing Fayol's enduring influence on management theory.

"Next," Dr. Hayes continued, "we have Max Weber's Bureaucratic Theory."

As he spoke, images of Weber's seminal work filled the screen, depicting the rational-legal authority structure he proposed.

"Weber argued that a rational-legal authority structure, characterized by clear rules, impersonality, and merit-based advancement, was the most efficient way to organize large-scale organizations," Dr. Hayes explained. "His ideas laid the foundation for modern bureaucratic systems, influencing everything from government agencies to multinational corporations."

A hand went up from a student named Marcus. "How did Weber's theories differ from Taylor's?"

"Another excellent question," Dr. Hayes said. "While Taylor focused primarily on efficiency and productivity at the individual level, Weber took a broader view, examining the organizational structures and processes that underpin effective governance. Both theorists contributed invaluable insights to the field of public administration, albeit from different perspectives."

He paused, allowing the students a moment to absorb the information before continuing.

"Finally," Dr. Hayes said, "we have Mary Parker Follett's contributions to administrative theory."

As he spoke, images of Follett's pioneering work filled the screen, depicting her groundbreaking ideas on organizational dynamics and group behavior.

"Follett's work focused on the importance of human relations in organizations," Dr. Hayes explained. "She emphasized the interconnectedness of individuals within groups and advocated for collaborative decision-making and conflict resolution."

A student named Jason raised his hand. "How did Follett's theories differ from those of her contemporaries?"

"Another astute question," Dr. Hayes replied. "While Taylor, Fayol, and Weber focused primarily on hierarchical structures and formal authority, Follett recognized the importance of informal networks and interpersonal relationships in organizational dynamics. Her ideas laid the groundwork for modern theories of organizational behavior and management."

As the lecture drew to a close, Dr. Hayes summarized the key points for his students, reminding them of the enduring relevance of the classical theories of administration.

"As we move forward in our exploration of public administration," he said, "remember the foundational principles laid down by Taylor, Fayol, Weber, and Follett. Their ideas continue to shape the way we think about governance and management, providing valuable insights into the complexities of organizational dynamics."

The students left the lecture hall, their minds buzzing with newfound knowledge and appreciation for the historical roots of their field. Dr. Hayes watched them go, feeling a sense of satisfaction at having sparked their curiosity and laid the groundwork for their continued exploration of public administration.

Bureaucratic Theory and Its Critiques

Dr. Robert Hayes adjusted his glasses, ready to delve into the complexities of bureaucratic theory and its critiques. This part of the lecture promised to be particularly engaging, as students often had strong opinions about the merits and shortcomings of bureaucracy in modern governance.

"Good morning, class," Dr. Hayes greeted, his voice resonating with anticipation. "Today, we continue our exploration of the theoretical foundations of public administration with a deep dive into bureaucratic theory and its critiques."

He clicked to the first slide, displaying the title: "Bureaucratic Theory."

"Bureaucratic theory, as proposed by Max Weber, has had a profound impact on the structure and functioning of modern organizations," Dr. Hayes began. "Weber argued that a rational-legal authority structure, characterized by clear rules, impersonality, and merit-based advancement, was the most efficient way to organize large-scale organizations."

As he spoke, images of Weber's seminal work filled the screen, depicting the hierarchical structures and formal procedures he proposed.

"Bureaucratic systems," Dr. Hayes continued, "are characterized by division of labor, hierarchy of authority, formal rules and procedures, impersonality, and career advancement based on merit."

A hand shot up from a student named Emily. "What are some examples of bureaucratic systems in public administration?"

"Great question, Emily," Dr. Hayes replied. "Government agencies, such as the Internal Revenue Service (IRS) or the

Social Security Administration (SSA), are classic examples of bureaucratic systems. They have clear hierarchies, formal rules and procedures, and standardized processes for decision-making and resource allocation."

He clicked to the next slide, which read: "Critiques of Bureaucratic Theory."

"While bureaucratic systems have their strengths," Dr. Hayes explained, "they are not without their criticisms. Over the years, scholars and practitioners have identified several drawbacks to bureaucratic organizations."

The slide displayed a list of critiques, including rigidity, inefficiency, red tape, lack of flexibility, and resistance to change.

"Perhaps the most common critique of bureaucratic systems is their perceived rigidity and inflexibility," Dr. Hayes said. "Bureaucracies are often slow to adapt to changing circumstances, leading to inefficiencies and delays in decision-making."

A student named Marcus raised his hand. "How do bureaucracies contribute to red tape?"

"An excellent question, Marcus," Dr. Hayes replied. "Red tape refers to excessive bureaucracy or administrative procedures that impede efficiency and effectiveness. Bureaucracies, with their emphasis on rules and procedures, can sometimes become bogged down in red tape, hindering their ability to deliver services in a timely manner."

He clicked to the next slide, which displayed a graph depicting the growth of bureaucracy over time.

"Another critique of bureaucratic systems," Dr. Hayes continued, "is their tendency to expand in size and scope over time. As organizations grow, they often become more complex and bureaucratic, leading to increased inefficiencies and administrative costs."

A hand went up from a student named Jessica. "How can bureaucracies address these critiques?"

"An excellent question, Jessica," Dr. Hayes replied. "While bureaucratic systems have their drawbacks, they also have strengths, such as stability, predictability, and accountability. To address the critiques, bureaucracies can implement reforms to streamline processes, increase transparency, and encourage innovation and flexibility."

He paused, allowing the students to absorb the information before continuing.

"Despite their criticisms," Dr. Hayes said, "bureaucratic systems remain an integral part of modern governance. Understanding their strengths and weaknesses is essential for anyone working in public administration."

As the lecture drew to a close, Dr. Hayes summarized the key points for his students, reminding them of the nuanced nature of bureaucratic theory and its critiques.

"As you continue your studies," he said, "remember to critically evaluate bureaucratic systems and consider how they can be improved to better serve the needs of society."

The students left the lecture hall, their minds buzzing with questions and ideas. Dr. Hayes watched them go, feeling a sense of satisfaction at having sparked their curiosity and challenged their assumptions about bureaucracy in modern governance.

New Public Management (NPM)

Dr. Robert Hayes stood at the front of the lecture hall, ready to explore the transformative ideas of New Public Management (NPM). This topic always sparked lively discussions, as students grappled with the implications of introducing private sector principles into public administration.

"Good morning, class," Dr. Hayes greeted, his voice carrying a note of excitement. "Today, we dive into the realm of New Public Management, a paradigm shift that revolutionized the way we think about governance and public administration."

He clicked to the first slide, displaying the title: "New Public Management."

"New Public Management emerged in the late 20th century as a response to the perceived inefficiencies of traditional bureaucratic systems," Dr. Hayes began. "It advocated for the application of private sector principles to improve the efficiency, effectiveness, and responsiveness of public services."

As he spoke, images of key NPM thinkers filled the screen, illustrating their ground-breaking ideas.

"The central tenets of NPM include decentralization, competition, performance measurement, and customer orientation," Dr. Hayes explained. "Proponents argued that introducing market-like mechanisms into public administration would incentivize efficiency and innovation."

A hand shot up from a student named Emily. "How does NPM differ from traditional bureaucratic systems?"

"An excellent question, Emily," Dr. Hayes replied. "While traditional bureaucracies are characterized by hierarchical structures, standardized procedures, and centralized decision-making, NPM emphasizes flexibility, accountability, and results-oriented management."

He clicked to the next slide, which read: "Key Features of New Public Management."

"Let's explore some of the key features of NPM," Dr. Hayes continued. "First, decentralization. NPM advocates for delegating decision-making authority to lower levels of government or even non-governmental organizations, allowing for greater responsiveness to local needs."

A student named Marcus raised his hand. "How does decentralization improve public services?"

"Decentralization can lead to more responsive and tailored services," Dr. Hayes explained. "By empowering local authorities or service providers to make decisions, governments can better address the unique needs of their communities and foster innovation."

He clicked to the next slide, which displayed the phrase: "Competition and Market Mechanisms."

"Another key feature of NPM is the introduction of competition and market mechanisms," Dr. Hayes said. "Proponents argued that introducing competition into public services would incentivize efficiency and drive innovation."

A hand went up from a student named Jessica. "What are some examples of competition in public services?"

"Great question, Jessica," Dr. Hayes replied. "Examples include the introduction of competitive tendering for government contracts, privatization of public services, and the use of performance-based contracting. By introducing competition, governments aim to improve service quality and reduce costs."

He clicked to the next slide, which displayed the phrase: "Performance Measurement and Accountability."

"NPM also emphasizes the importance of performance measurement and accountability," Dr. Hayes explained. "Governments are encouraged to set clear performance targets, measure outcomes, and hold public servants accountable for results."

A student named Alex raised his hand. "How does performance measurement improve public services?"

"Performance measurement allows governments to assess the effectiveness of their policies and programs," Dr. Hayes replied. "By tracking key performance indicators, governments can identify areas for improvement, allocate resources more effectively, and ensure that public services meet the needs of citizens."

He clicked to the next slide, which displayed the phrase: "Customer Orientation."

"Finally, NPM promotes a customer-oriented approach to public service delivery," Dr. Hayes said. "Governments are encouraged to treat citizens as customers and focus on meeting their needs and preferences."

A hand shot up from a student named Brian. "How does a customer-oriented approach differ from traditional public service delivery?"

"Traditionally, public services were designed and delivered based on bureaucratic processes and procedures," Dr. Hayes explained. "A customer-oriented approach, on the other hand, focuses on responsiveness, accessibility, and user satisfaction. It emphasizes listening to citizens' feedback and adapting services to meet their evolving needs."

As the lecture drew to a close, Dr. Hayes summarized the key points for his students, reminding them of the transformative potential of New Public Management in modern governance.

"As you continue your studies," he said, "consider the implications of NPM for public administration and the ongoing debate surrounding its effectiveness and drawbacks."

The students left the lecture hall, their minds buzzing with questions and ideas. Dr. Hayes watched them go, feeling a sense of satisfaction at having introduced them to the dynamic world of New Public Management and its impact on the field of public administration.

Governance and Network Theory

Dr. Robert Hayes stood before his class, eager to delve into the complexities of governance and network theory. This topic always sparked intrigue among his students, as it challenged traditional notions of hierarchical decision-making and introduced the concept of collaborative governance.

"Good morning, class," Dr. Hayes greeted, his voice projecting warmth and enthusiasm. "Today, we embark on a fascinating journey into the realms of governance and network theory, exploring the ways in which power and authority are distributed and exercised in modern societies."

He clicked to the first slide, displaying the title: "Governance and Network Theory."

"Governance refers to the processes and structures through which decisions are made and implemented in society," Dr. Hayes began. "Traditionally, governance was associated with formal government institutions and hierarchical structures. However, in recent years, scholars have expanded the concept to include a broader range of actors and mechanisms."

As he spoke, images of interconnected networks filled the screen, illustrating the complex web of relationships that characterize modern governance.

"Network theory," Dr. Hayes continued, "emphasizes the interconnectedness of actors and organizations in the governance process. It views governance as a collaborative endeavor involving multiple stakeholders, including government agencies, non-profit organizations, private sector entities, and civil society groups."

A hand shot up from a student named Emily. "How does network theory differ from traditional hierarchical governance?"

"An excellent question, Emily," Dr. Hayes replied. "Traditional hierarchical governance is characterized by clear lines of authority and decision-making, with power concentrated at the top of the hierarchy. Network theory, on the other hand, recognizes the importance of horizontal relationships and informal networks in shaping policy outcomes."

He clicked to the next slide, which read: "Key Features of Network Governance."

"Let's explore some of the key features of network governance," Dr. Hayes said. "First, it emphasizes collaboration and cooperation among diverse stakeholders. Instead of top-down decision-making, network governance relies on dialogue, negotiation, and consensus-building."

A student named Marcus raised his hand. "How does collaboration improve policy outcomes?"

"Collaboration allows for the pooling of resources, expertise, and perspectives," Dr. Hayes explained. "By bringing together a diverse range of stakeholders, governments can develop more informed and effective policies that reflect the needs and interests of all involved parties."

He clicked to the next slide, which displayed the phrase:

"Decentralization and Flexibility."

"Another key feature of network governance is decentralization and flexibility," Dr. Hayes continued. "Instead of rigid hierarchical structures, network governance allows for greater flexibility and adaptability in responding to complex and dynamic challenges."

A hand went up from a student named Jessica. "How does decentralization contribute to flexibility in governance?"

"Decentralization allows decision-making authority to be dispersed among multiple actors and organizations," Dr. Hayes replied. "This enables more agile responses to local needs and conditions, as decision-makers are closer to the ground and better able to tailor policies to specific contexts."

He clicked to the next slide, which displayed the phrase: "Inclusivity and Participation."

"Network governance also emphasizes inclusivity and participation," Dr. Hayes said. "By involving a wide range of stakeholders in the decision-making process, governments can ensure that policies reflect the diverse perspectives and interests of the communities they serve."

A hand shot up from a student named Alex. "How can governments ensure inclusivity in network governance?"

"Governments can promote inclusivity through mechanisms such as public consultations, citizen panels, and participatory decision-making processes," Dr. Hayes replied. "By actively engaging with stakeholders, governments can build trust, foster collaboration, and improve the legitimacy of their decisions."

As the lecture drew to a close, Dr. Hayes summarized the key points for his students, reminding them of the transformative potential of network governance in modern societies.

"As you continue your studies," he said, "consider the implications of network theory for public administration and the ways in which collaborative governance can enhance the effectiveness and legitimacy of government decision-making."

The students left the lecture hall, their minds buzzing with questions and ideas. Dr. Hayes watched them go, feeling a sense of satisfaction at having introduced them to the dynamic world of governance and network theory and its impact on the field of public administration.

Public Choice Theory

Dr. Robert Hayes paced the front of the lecture hall, eager to engage his students in a discussion on public choice theory. This topic often sparked debate, as it challenged traditional views of government decision-making and introduced economic principles into the realm of public administration.

"Good morning, class," Dr. Hayes greeted, his voice carrying a tone of excitement. "Today, we explore the intriguing world of public choice theory, which applies economic principles to the study of political decision-making."

He clicked to the first slide, displaying the title: "Public Choice Theory."

"Public choice theory," Dr. Hayes began, "posits that individuals, including elected officials and bureaucrats, act in their own self-interest when making decisions in the public sphere. It challenges the notion of benevolent government and highlights the role of incentives in shaping behavior."

As he spoke, images of economists and political scientists filled the screen, illustrating the interdisciplinary nature of public choice theory.

"The central premise of public choice theory," Dr. Hayes continued, "is that individuals seek to maximize their own utility or welfare, whether they are voters, politicians, or bureaucrats. This self-interested behavior can lead to outcomes that may not always align with the public interest."

A hand shot up from a student named Emily. "How does public choice theory differ from traditional views of government decision-making?"

"An excellent question, Emily," Dr. Hayes replied. "Traditionally, government decision-making was often viewed through the lens of benevolent policymakers seeking to maximize social welfare. Public choice theory, however, challenges this notion by emphasizing the self-interested nature of human behavior and the importance of incentives in shaping decision-making."

He clicked to the next slide, which read: "Key Concepts of Public Choice Theory."

"Let's explore some of the key concepts of public choice theory," Dr. Hayes said. "First, we have the concept of rational self-interest. Public choice theorists argue that individuals, including politicians and bureaucrats, act rationally to maximize their own utility or welfare."

A student named Marcus raised his hand. "How do politicians and bureaucrats pursue their self-interest in the public sphere?"

"Politicians may seek to maximize their chances of reelection by pursuing policies that appeal to their constituents or special interest groups," Dr. Hayes explained. "Bureaucrats may seek to expand their budgets or influence by advocating for policies that benefit their agency or career advancement."

He clicked to the next slide, which displayed the phrase:

"Incentives Matter."

"Another key concept of public choice theory is that incentives matter," Dr. Hayes continued. "Individuals respond to incentives, whether they are financial rewards, career advancement opportunities, or reelection prospects."

A hand went up from a student named Jessica. "How do incentives influence government decision-making?"

"Incentives can influence government decision-making in various ways," Dr. Hayes replied. "For example, politicians may prioritize policies that are popular with their constituents or special interest groups to increase their chances of re-election. Bureaucrats may seek to expand their budgets or influence by advocating for policies that benefit their agency or career advancement."

He clicked to the next slide, which displayed the phrase: "Public Choice and Policy Outcomes."

"Finally, public choice theory suggests that government policies and outcomes are often the result of political bargaining and compromise," Dr. Hayes said. "Rather than reflecting the public interest, policies may reflect the interests of powerful groups or individuals who have the most influence over the decision-making process."

As the lecture drew to a close, Dr. Hayes summarized the key points for his students, reminding them of the transformative potential of public choice theory in understanding government decision-making.

"As you continue your studies," he said, "consider the implications of public choice theory for public administration and the ways in which incentives shape government policies and outcomes."

The students left the lecture hall, their minds buzzing with questions and ideas. Dr. Hayes watched them go, feeling a sense of satisfaction at having introduced them to the dynamic world of public choice theory and its impact on the field of public administration.

Comparative Public Administration

Dr. Robert Hayes stood before his class, ready to explore the intricacies of comparative public administration. This topic always fascinated his students, as it offered a glimpse into the diverse approaches to governance adopted by countries around the world.

"Good morning, class," Dr. Hayes greeted, his voice resonating with enthusiasm. "Today, we embark on an exciting journey into the realm of comparative public administration, where we examine the similarities and differences in administrative systems across different countries."

He clicked to the first slide, displaying the title: "Comparative Public Administration."

"Comparative public administration," Dr. Hayes began, "is the study of administrative systems, practices, and policies in different countries. It seeks to understand how factors such as history, culture, and political context shape the structure and functioning of government."

As he spoke, images of diverse administrative systems filled the screen, illustrating the rich tapestry of governance models around the world.

"The central goal of comparative public administration," Dr. Hayes continued, "is to identify best practices, learn from successful experiences, and promote cross-cultural understanding in the field of public administration."

A hand shot up from a student named Emily. "How does comparative public administration contribute to the study of public administration?"

"An excellent question, Emily," Dr. Hayes replied. "Comparative public administration allows us to gain insights into the strengths and weaknesses of different administrative systems, as well as the factors that contribute to their success or failure. By comparing administrative practices across countries, we can identify innovative approaches and adapt them to our own context."

He clicked to the next slide, which read: "Key Concepts of Comparative Public Administration."

"Let's explore some of the key concepts of comparative public administration," Dr. Hayes said. "First, we have the concept of administrative cultures. Administrative cultures refer to the values, norms, and practices that shape the behavior of public officials in different countries."

A student named Marcus raised his hand. "How do administrative cultures differ across countries?"

"Administrative cultures can vary significantly from one country to another," Dr. Hayes explained. "For example, some countries may have a culture of hierarchy and formalism, where adherence to rules and procedures is highly valued. Others may have a more flexible and adaptive culture, where innovation and creativity are encouraged."

He clicked to the next slide, which displayed the phrase: "Institutional Design."

"Another key concept of comparative public administration is institutional design," Dr. Hayes continued. "Institutional design refers to the structure and organization of government institutions, including the distribution of powers, responsibilities, and resources."

A hand went up from a student named Jessica. "How does institutional design affect government performance?"

"Institutional design can have a significant impact on government performance," Dr. Hayes replied. "For example, countries with decentralized systems of government may be better able to respond to local needs and preferences, while countries with centralized systems may be more efficient in resource allocation and decision-making."

He clicked to the next slide, which displayed the phrase: "Policy Transfer and Lesson Drawing."

"Finally, comparative public administration emphasizes the importance of policy transfer and lesson drawing," Dr. Hayes said. "Policy transfer involves the adoption of policies, practices, or reforms from one country to another. Lesson drawing involves learning from the experiences of other countries and applying those lessons to one's own context."

As the lecture drew to a close, Dr. Hayes summarized the key points for his students, reminding them of the transformative potential of comparative public administration in promoting cross-cultural understanding and improving government performance.

"As you continue your studies," he said, "consider the implications of comparative public administration for public administration and the ways in which cross-national comparisons can inform policy-making and institutional reform."

The students left the lecture hall, their minds buzzing with questions and ideas. Dr. Hayes watched them go, feeling a sense of satisfaction at having introduced them to the dynamic world of comparative public administration and its impact on the field of public administration.

3

Chapter 3: Organizational Structure and Design

Types of Organizations

Dr. Robert Hayes entered the classroom with a sense of anticipation, ready to guide his students through an exploration of organizational structure and design. Today's topic, the different types of organizations, promised to be particularly enlightening as it laid the foundation for understanding the intricacies of governance.

"Good morning, class," Dr. Hayes greeted, his voice projecting warmth and enthusiasm. "Today, we embark on a journey into the world of organizational structure and design, where we'll explore the various types of organizations that exist in the realm of public administration."

He clicked to the first slide, displaying the title: "Types of Organizations."

"Organizations," Dr. Hayes began, "come in many shapes and sizes, each with its own unique characteristics and functions. Understanding the different types of organizations is essential for grasping how they operate within the broader context of governance."

As he spoke, images of various organizational structures filled the screen, illustrating the diversity of forms that organizations can take.

"The first type of organization we'll explore is the hierarchical organization," Dr. Hayes continued. "Hierarchical organizations are characterized by clear lines of authority and a vertical chain of command. Decision-making authority flows from top to bottom, with each level of the hierarchy responsible for specific tasks and functions."

A hand shot up from a student named Emily. "Can you give us an example of a hierarchical organization in public administration?"

"Of course, Emily," Dr. Hayes replied. "Government agencies, such as the Department of Education or the Environmental Protection Agency, are classic examples of hierarchical organizations. They have a clear organizational structure with departments, divisions, and units, each responsible for carrying out specific functions."

He clicked to the next slide, which read: "Matrix Organizations."

"Next, we have matrix organizations," Dr. Hayes continued. "Matrix organizations are characterized by a combination of functional and project-based structures. Employees report to both functional managers and project managers, resulting in a more flexible and dynamic work environment."

A student named Marcus raised his hand. "How do matrix organizations differ from hierarchical organizations?"

"Great question, Marcus," Dr. Hayes replied. "In hierarchical organizations, authority flows vertically, with each level of the hierarchy responsible for specific tasks. In matrix organizations, however, authority can flow both vertically and horizontally, with employees belonging to multiple teams or projects."

He clicked to the next slide, which displayed the phrase: "Network Organizations."

"Finally, we have network organizations," Dr. Hayes said. "Network organizations are characterized by decentralized decision-making and a focus on collaboration and partnerships. They often consist of a network of interconnected stakeholders, including government agencies, non-profit organizations, and private sector entities."

A hand went up from a student named Jessica. "How do network organizations function in practice?"

"Network organizations rely on collaboration and partnership to achieve their goals," Dr. Hayes explained. "Rather than relying solely on internal resources and capabilities, they leverage the expertise and resources of external partners to address complex challenges and deliver services more effectively."

As the lecture drew to a close, Dr. Hayes summarized the key points for his students, reminding them of the importance of understanding the different types of organizations in public administration.

"As you continue your studies," he said, "consider how organizational structure and design impact the effectiveness and efficiency of public administration, and how different types of organizations can be leveraged to achieve organizational goals."

The students left the lecture hall, their minds buzzing

with questions and ideas. Dr. Hayes watched them go, feeling a sense of satisfaction at having laid the foundation for their understanding of organizational structure and design in public administration.

Principles of Organizational Structure

Dr. Robert Hayes stood before his class, ready to delve deeper into the principles of organizational structure. This topic was fundamental to understanding how organizations function and how their structures impact their effectiveness.

"Good morning, class," Dr. Hayes greeted, his voice filled with enthusiasm. "Today, we continue our exploration of organizational structure and design by examining the principles that underpin how organizations are structured."

He clicked to the first slide, displaying the title: "Principles of Organizational Structure."

"Organizational structure," Dr. Hayes began, "refers to the framework of roles, responsibilities, and relationships that determine how an organization operates. The principles of organizational structure provide guidance on how to design effective and efficient organizations."

As he spoke, images of organizational charts and diagrams filled the screen, illustrating the various elements of organizational structure.

"The first principle of organizational structure is clarity of roles and responsibilities," Dr. Hayes continued. "In order for an organization to function effectively, it is essential that each member understands their role and responsibilities within the organization."

A hand shot up from a student named Emily. "How can

organizations ensure clarity of roles and responsibilities?"

"Excellent question, Emily," Dr. Hayes replied. "Organizations can ensure clarity of roles and responsibilities through job descriptions, organizational charts, and clear lines of authority. By clearly defining expectations and responsibilities, organizations can minimize confusion and maximize productivity."

He clicked to the next slide, which read: "Hierarchy and Span of Control."

"The second principle of organizational structure is hierarchy and span of control," Dr. Hayes explained. "Hierarchy refers to the levels of authority within an organization, with higher levels having authority over lower levels. Span of control refers to the number of subordinates that a manager or supervisor can effectively oversee."

A student named Marcus raised his hand. "How does hierarchy and span of control impact organizational effectiveness?"

"Hierarchy and span of control can impact organizational effectiveness in several ways," Dr. Hayes replied. "A clear hierarchy can provide clarity of authority and decision-making, while an appropriate span of control can ensure that managers are able to effectively supervise their subordinates without becoming overwhelmed."

He clicked to the next slide, which displayed the phrase: "Unity of Command."

"The third principle of organizational structure is unity of command," Dr. Hayes continued. "Unity of command means that each employee should receive orders from only one supervisor. This helps to avoid confusion and conflicting instructions."

A hand went up from a student named Jessica. "How does

unity of command contribute to organizational efficiency?"

"Unity of command ensures that employees receive clear and consistent instructions," Dr. Hayes explained. "By avoiding conflicting orders, organizations can minimize confusion and increase productivity. Employees know who they report to and who is responsible for their performance."

As the lecture drew to a close, Dr. Hayes summarized the key points for his students, reminding them of the importance of principles of organizational structure in designing effective and efficient organizations.

"As you continue your studies," he said, "consider how these principles can be applied in practice to improve organizational effectiveness and achieve organizational goals."

The students left the lecture hall, their minds buzzing with newfound knowledge about the principles of organizational structure. Dr. Hayes watched them go, feeling a sense of satisfaction at having deepened their understanding of this fundamental aspect of public administration.

Centralization vs. Decentralization

Dr. Robert Hayes entered the classroom with a sense of anticipation, ready to explore the dynamic interplay between centralization and decentralization in organizational structure. This topic always sparked lively discussions among his students, as it touched upon fundamental questions of power and decision-making within organizations.

"Good morning, class," Dr. Hayes greeted, his voice resonating with energy. "Today, we delve into the fascinating topic of centralization and decentralization, examining the different approaches to distributing authority within organizations."

He clicked to the first slide, displaying the title: "Centralization vs. Decentralization."

"Centralization," Dr. Hayes began, "refers to the concentration of decision-making authority at the top levels of an organization. In centralized organizations, key decisions are made by a few individuals or a central governing body."

As he spoke, images contrasting centralized and decentralized organizational structures filled the screen, illustrating the differences in decision-making processes.

"The advantages of centralization include streamlined decision-making, consistency in policy implementation, and the ability to respond quickly to changing conditions," Dr. Hayes continued. "However, centralization can also lead to bureaucratic inertia, stifling innovation and creativity."

A hand shot up from a student named Emily. "How does centralization impact employee morale and motivation?"

"An excellent question, Emily," Dr. Hayes replied. "Centralization can lead to feelings of disempowerment and lack of autonomy among employees, which can negatively impact morale and motivation. Employees may feel that their voices are not heard and that they have little control over their work."

He clicked to the next slide, which read: "Decentralization."

"On the other hand," Dr. Hayes continued, "decentralization refers to the dispersion of decision-making authority throughout an organization. In decentralized organizations, decision-making authority is pushed down to lower levels, empowering employees to make decisions that affect their work."

A student named Marcus raised his hand. "What are the benefits of decentralization?"

"Decentralization has several advantages," Dr. Hayes explained. "It promotes employee empowerment and engagement, as employees feel more involved in the decision-making process. Decentralization can also foster innovation and creativity, as employees at lower levels are closer to the ground and may have better insights into local conditions."

He clicked to the next slide, which displayed the phrase: "Finding the Right Balance."

"Finding the right balance between centralization and decentralization is key," Dr. Hayes said. "There is no one-size-fits-all approach, and the optimal degree of centralization or decentralization will depend on factors such as organizational size, complexity, and external environment."

A hand went up from a student named Jessica. "How can organizations determine the appropriate level of centralization or decentralization?"

"Organizations can determine the appropriate level of centralization or decentralization through careful analysis of their goals, resources, and external environment," Dr. Hayes replied. "They should consider factors such as the need for consistency and standardization, the importance of local knowledge and innovation, and the capacity of employees to make informed decisions."

As the lecture drew to a close, Dr. Hayes summarized the key points for his students, reminding them of the importance of finding the right balance between centralization and decentralization in organizational structure.

"As you continue your studies," he said, "consider how centralization and decentralization can be leveraged to promote organizational effectiveness and achieve strategic goals."

The students left the lecture hall, their minds buzzing with newfound insights into the dynamics of decision-making within organizations. Dr. Hayes watched them go, feeling a sense of fulfillment at having sparked their curiosity and deepened their understanding of organizational structure and design.

Organizational Culture and Public Values

Dr. Robert Hayes entered the classroom, prepared to delve into the fascinating realm of organizational culture and public values. This topic was crucial for understanding the underlying beliefs and norms that shape the behavior of individuals within organizations and their alignment with the broader values of society.

"Good morning, class," Dr. Hayes greeted, his voice resonating with enthusiasm. "Today, we explore the intricate relationship between organizational culture and public values, and how they influence the functioning of public administration."

He clicked to the first slide, displaying the title: "Organizational Culture and Public Values."

"Organizational culture," Dr. Hayes began, "refers to the shared beliefs, values, and norms that shape the behavior and interactions of individuals within an organization. Public values, on the other hand, are the principles and ideals that guide the actions of public servants and inform the decisions of government."

As he spoke, images depicting diverse organizational cultures and public values filled the screen, illustrating the complexity of their interplay.

"The organizational culture of a public agency," Dr. Hayes continued, "plays a significant role in shaping its operations, decision-making processes, and interactions with stakeholders. It reflects the collective identity of the organization and influences how employees perceive their roles and responsibilities."

A hand shot up from a student named Emily. "How does organizational culture impact the effectiveness of public administration?"

"Organizational culture can have a profound impact on the effectiveness of public administration," Dr. Hayes replied. "A strong and positive organizational culture can foster collaboration, innovation, and commitment among employees, leading to improved performance and service delivery. Conversely, a toxic or dysfunctional culture can undermine morale, productivity, and public trust."

He clicked to the next slide, which read: "Alignment with Public Values."

"Public organizations," Dr. Hayes continued, "are expected to uphold and advance public values such as accountability, transparency, integrity, and responsiveness. The alignment between organizational culture and public values is essential for ensuring that public servants act ethically and in the public interest."

A student named Marcus raised his hand. "How can organizations ensure that their culture aligns with public values?"

"Organizations can promote alignment with public values through leadership, communication, and organizational practices," Dr. Hayes explained. "Leadership sets the tone for organizational culture and should exemplify the values they seek to promote. Communication channels should be open and transparent, allowing for dialogue and feedback. Organizational practices, such as performance evaluations and reward systems, should reinforce desired behaviors and values."

He clicked to the next slide, which displayed the phrase: "Fostering a Culture of Service."

"Ultimately," Dr. Hayes said, "fostering a culture of service is essential for public organizations to fulfill their mission and serve the needs of the public effectively. This requires a commitment to ethical conduct, accountability, and continuous improvement."

As the lecture drew to a close, Dr. Hayes summarized the key points for his students, emphasizing the importance of organizational culture and its alignment with public values in public administration.

"As you continue your studies," he said, "consider how organizational culture can be shaped and nurtured to promote ethical behavior, enhance performance, and uphold the public trust."

The students left the lecture hall, their minds buzzing with newfound insights into the role of organizational culture in public administration. Dr. Hayes watched them go, feeling a sense of fulfillment at having sparked their curiosity and deepened their understanding of this critical aspect of organizational structure and design.

Leadership in Public Organizations

Dr. Robert Hayes stepped into the classroom, ready to explore the crucial role of leadership in public organizations. This topic was fundamental for understanding how leaders shape organizational culture, inspire their teams, and navigate the complexities of public administration.

"Good morning, class," Dr. Hayes greeted, his voice exuding warmth and authority. "Today, we delve into the dynamic world of leadership in public organizations, examining the qualities and practices that define effective leadership in the realm of public administration."

He clicked to the first slide, displaying the title: "Leadership in Public Organizations."

"Leadership," Dr. Hayes began, "is the process of influencing and guiding others to achieve common goals. In public organizations, effective leadership is essential for inspiring public servants, fostering innovation, and driving positive change."

As he spoke, images of renowned public leaders and inspirational quotes filled the screen, illustrating the diversity of leadership styles and approaches.

"The role of leadership in public organizations," Dr. Hayes continued, "extends beyond traditional management functions to encompass vision-setting, strategic planning, and stakeholder engagement. Public leaders must navigate complex political environments, ethical dilemmas, and public scrutiny while upholding the values of public service."

A hand shot up from a student named Emily. "What are the key qualities of effective leadership in public organizations?"

"An excellent question, Emily," Dr. Hayes replied. "Effective leaders in public organizations demonstrate several key qualities, including integrity, empathy, resilience, and strategic vision. They inspire trust and confidence among their team members, foster collaboration and innovation, and advocate for the public interest."

He clicked to the next slide, which read: "Transformational Leadership."

"One of the most influential leadership theories in public administration is transformational leadership," Dr. Hayes explained. "Transformational leaders inspire and motivate their followers to achieve higher levels of performance by appealing to their values and emotions. They articulate a compelling vision, empower their team members, and lead by example."

A student named Marcus raised his hand. "How can leaders foster a culture of innovation in public organizations?"

"Leaders can foster a culture of innovation by encouraging creativity, risk-taking, and experimentation," Dr. Hayes replied. "They can create opportunities for cross-functional collaboration, provide resources and support for innovative projects, and celebrate successes. By fostering a culture of innovation, leaders can position their organizations to adapt and thrive in an ever-changing environment."

He clicked to the next slide, which displayed the phrase: "Ethical Leadership."

"Ethical leadership is another critical aspect of effective leadership in public organizations," Dr. Hayes said. "Ethical leaders demonstrate honesty, transparency, and accountability in their actions, and they prioritize the public interest above personal gain. They set high ethical standards for themselves and their team members and hold themselves accountable for their decisions and actions."

As the lecture drew to a close, Dr. Hayes summarized the key points for his students, reminding them of the importance of effective leadership in public organizations.

"As you continue your studies," he said, "consider the qualities and practices of effective leadership and how they contribute to organizational success and the advancement of the public interest."

The students left the lecture hall, their minds buzzing with newfound insights into the role of leadership in public organizations. Dr. Hayes watched them go, feeling a sense of satisfaction at having inspired and empowered the next generation of public leaders.

Case Studies of Organizational Designs

Dr. Robert Hayes paced in front of the class, eager to delve into real-world examples of organizational designs in public administration. Case studies offered invaluable insights into the application of theoretical concepts and principles in practice, sparking lively discussions among his students.

"Good morning, class," Dr. Hayes greeted, his voice brimming with enthusiasm. "Today, we turn our attention to case studies of organizational designs, exploring how different public organizations have structured themselves to meet their unique challenges and objectives."

He clicked to the first slide, displaying the title: "Case Studies of Organizational Designs."

"Case studies provide us with rich examples of how organizational theory is applied in real-world settings," Dr. Hayes began. "We'll examine the organizational structures, cultures, and leadership approaches of various public organizations to understand their successes, challenges, and lessons learned."

As he spoke, images of diverse public organizations, from government agencies to non-profit organizations, filled the screen, setting the stage for the upcoming case studies.

"Our first case study," Dr. Hayes continued, "takes us to the Department of Health and Human Services (DHHS), a large federal agency responsible for protecting the health and well-being of all Americans. DHHS faces complex challenges ranging from healthcare delivery to social services provision."

A hand shot up from a student named Emily. "How does DHHS structure itself to address such diverse challenges?"

"Great question, Emily," Dr. Hayes replied. "DHHS utilizes a hierarchical organizational structure with multiple operating divisions and offices, each responsible for specific functions such as public health, Medicaid, and child welfare. This structure allows for centralized coordination and oversight while also providing flexibility for specialized functions."

He clicked to the next slide, which displayed an organizational chart of DHHS.

"Our next case study," Dr. Hayes continued, "takes us to the New York City Department of Transportation (NYCDOT), a municipal agency responsible for the planning, operation, and maintenance of the city's transportation infrastructure."

A student named Marcus raised his hand. "How does NYCDOT ensure coordination and collaboration across different modes of transportation?"

"NYCDOT employs a matrix organizational structure," Dr. Hayes explained, "with functional units responsible for areas such as road maintenance, public transit, and traffic management, as well as project teams focused on specific initiatives such as bike lanes or pedestrian safety. This structure allows for both functional expertise and cross-functional collaboration."

He clicked to the next slide, which displayed an organizational chart of NYCDOT.

"Our final case study," Dr. Hayes said, "takes us to a non-profit organization, Save the Environment Foundation (SEF), dedicated to environmental conservation and advocacy."

A hand went up from a student named Jessica. "How does SEF leverage its organizational culture to drive its mission?"

"SEF fosters a culture of environmental stewardship and activism," Dr. Hayes replied. "Employees are passionate about the organization's mission and values, which are reflected in their collaborative approach to problem-solving and their commitment to sustainability. This culture of shared purpose and dedication enables SEF to effectively advocate for environmental protection and mobilize support for its initiatives."

He clicked to the next slide, which displayed an organizational chart of SEF.

"As we analyze these case studies," Dr. Hayes concluded, "we'll consider the strengths and weaknesses of different organizational designs and their implications for public administration. By examining real-world examples, we gain valuable insights into the complexities of organizational structure and design in practice."

The students eagerly leaned forward, ready to dive into the case studies and uncover the lessons they held. Dr. Hayes smiled, knowing that these practical examples would deepen their understanding of organizational structure and design in public administration.

4

Chapter 4: Policy Making Process

Stages of Policy Making

D r. Robert Hayes entered the classroom with a sense of purpose, ready to guide his students through the intricate stages of the policy-making process. This topic was crucial for understanding how policies are formulated, implemented, and evaluated, shaping the landscape of governance.

"Good morning, class," Dr. Hayes greeted, his voice projecting authority and enthusiasm. "Today, we embark on a journey through the stages of the policy-making process, unraveling the complexities of how policies are crafted and enacted in the realm of public administration."

He clicked to the first slide, displaying the title: "Stages of Policy Making."

"The policy-making process," Dr. Hayes began, "is a dynamic and iterative process that involves multiple stages, each with its own set of actors, activities, and considerations."

As he spoke, images depicting the stages of policy making, from agenda setting to evaluation, filled the screen, setting the stage for the upcoming discussion.

"The first stage of the policy-making process is agenda setting," Dr. Hayes continued. "During this stage, issues are identified and prioritized for government action. This can be driven by various factors, including public opinion, media attention, and political leadership."

A hand shot up from a student named Emily. "How are issues selected for the policy agenda?"

"An excellent question, Emily," Dr. Hayes replied. "Issues may enter the policy agenda through various channels, such as public outcry, interest group advocacy, or government initiatives. The agenda-setting stage is characterized by competition and negotiation among different stakeholders to shape the policy agenda."

He clicked to the next slide, which read: "Policy Formulation."

"The next stage of the policy-making process is policy formulation," Dr. Hayes explained. "During this stage, policy options are developed, analyzed, and debated. This often involves gathering information, conducting research, and consulting with experts and stakeholders."

A student named Marcus raised his hand. "How do policymakers decide among competing policy options?"

"Policymakers must weigh various factors, including political feasibility, economic viability, and public support," Dr. Hayes replied. "They may also consider the values and priorities of the government, as well as the potential impact of the policy on different stakeholders. The policy formulation stage is characterized by compromise and negotiation as policymakers seek to craft policies that balance competing interests."

He clicked to the next slide, which displayed the phrase: "Policy Adoption."

"The third stage of the policy-making process is policy adoption," Dr. Hayes continued. "During this stage, the proposed policy is formally adopted by the government through legislation, regulation, or executive action. This often involves debate and deliberation in legislative bodies or administrative agencies."

A hand went up from a student named Jessica. "What factors influence the adoption of a policy?"

"The adoption of a policy is influenced by various factors, including political dynamics, public opinion, and interest group pressure," Dr. Hayes explained. "Policymakers must navigate these factors to garner support for their proposed policy and secure its passage or implementation."

As the lecture continued, Dr. Hayes guided his students through the remaining stages of the policy-making process, including implementation, evaluation, and feedback. Each stage offered its own challenges and opportunities, shaping the ultimate impact of policies on society.

"As you continue your studies," Dr. Hayes concluded, "consider the complexities of the policy-making process and the role of public administrators in navigating these challenges to craft effective and responsive policies."

The students left the lecture hall, their minds buzzing with newfound insights into the stages of the policy-making process. Dr. Hayes watched them go, feeling a sense of satisfaction at having illuminated this fundamental aspect of public administration.

Role of Public Administrators in Policy Development

Dr. Robert Hayes stood before his students, ready to explore the pivotal role of public administrators in the development of public policies. This aspect of the policy-making process was fundamental for understanding how policies are shaped and implemented on the ground, directly impacting the lives of citizens.

"Good morning, class," Dr. Hayes greeted, his voice filled with purpose. "Today, we delve into the role of public administrators in policy development, examining how they contribute to the formulation, implementation, and evaluation of public policies."

He clicked to the first slide, displaying the title: "Role of Public Administrators in Policy Development."

"Public administrators," Dr. Hayes began, "play a crucial role in every stage of the policy-making process, from agenda setting to evaluation. They are responsible for translating policy goals into actionable plans and ensuring that policies are effectively implemented and evaluated."

As he spoke, images of public administrators working in various government agencies and departments filled the screen, showcasing their diverse roles and responsibilities.

"The first stage of the policy-making process, agenda setting, often involves public administrators," Dr. Hayes continued. "They may conduct research, gather data, and analyze trends to identify emerging issues and inform policy priorities."

A hand shot up from a student named Emily. "How do public administrators contribute to policy formulation?"

"Public administrators contribute to policy formulation

by providing expertise, conducting analysis, and offering recommendations to policymakers," Dr. Hayes replied. "They may draft policy proposals, develop implementation plans, and assess the feasibility and impact of different policy options."

He clicked to the next slide, which read: "Policy Implementation."

"Policy implementation is where public administrators truly shine," Dr. Hayes explained. "They are responsible for translating policy directives into tangible actions and programs. This may involve coordinating with other government agencies, allocating resources, and overseeing the delivery of services to the public."

A student named Marcus raised his hand. "What challenges do public administrators face in policy implementation?"

"Policy implementation can be complex and challenging," Dr. Hayes acknowledged. "Public administrators must navigate bureaucratic obstacles, manage stakeholder expectations, and address unforeseen obstacles that may arise during implementation. Effective communication, collaboration, and problem-solving skills are essential for overcoming these challenges."

He clicked to the next slide, which displayed the phrase: "Policy Evaluation."

"The final stage of the policy-making process, policy evaluation, is critical for assessing the effectiveness and impact of policies," Dr. Hayes said. "Public administrators are responsible for conducting evaluations, analyzing data, and providing feedback to policymakers. This information is essential for refining existing policies, identifying areas for improvement, and informing future decision-making."

As the lecture continued, Dr. Hayes guided his students through the various roles and responsibilities of public administrators in policy development. From research and analysis to implementation and evaluation, public administrators played a central role in shaping and implementing public policies that served the needs of society.

"As you continue your studies," Dr. Hayes concluded, "consider the vital contributions that public administrators make to the policy-making process and the challenges they face in fulfilling their roles effectively."

The students left the lecture hall, their minds buzzing with newfound insights into the role of public administrators in policy development. Dr. Hayes watched them go, feeling a sense of pride in their growing understanding of this critical aspect of public administration.

Policy Analysis and Decision Making

Dr. Robert Hayes stood before his students, ready to delve into the intricacies of policy analysis and decision-making. This aspect of the policy-making process was crucial for understanding how policymakers evaluate different policy options and make informed decisions that impact the lives of citizens.

"Good morning, class," Dr. Hayes greeted, his voice filled with anticipation. "Today, we explore the critical role of policy analysis and decision-making in the policy-making process, examining how policymakers assess the feasibility, effectiveness, and implications of various policy options."

He clicked to the first slide, displaying the title: "Policy Analysis and Decision Making."

"Policy analysis," Dr. Hayes began, "is the process of systematically evaluating different policy options to inform decision-making. It involves gathering data, conducting research, and assessing the potential impact of policies on society."

As he spoke, images of policymakers poring over reports, data charts, and policy briefs filled the screen, illustrating the rigorous process of policy analysis.

"The first step in policy analysis is defining the problem," Dr. Hayes continued. "Policymakers must clearly understand the nature and scope of the issue they are addressing before they can develop effective policy solutions."

A hand shot up from a student named Emily. "How do policymakers gather the necessary data for policy analysis?"

"Policymakers gather data from various sources, including government agencies, research institutions, and stakeholder consultations," Dr. Hayes replied. "They may commission studies, conduct surveys, or analyze existing data sets to gain insights into the problem they are addressing and its underlying causes."

He clicked to the next slide, which read: "Policy Options Analysis."

"The next step in policy analysis is assessing different policy options," Dr. Hayes explained. "Policymakers evaluate the advantages, disadvantages, costs, and benefits of each option to determine which is most likely to achieve their policy goals."

A student named Marcus raised his hand. "How do policymakers weigh the trade-offs between different policy options?"

"Policymakers must consider various factors, including economic considerations, social impacts, and political feasibility,"

Dr. Hayes replied. "They may use tools such as cost-benefit analysis, risk assessment, and stakeholder analysis to evaluate the trade-offs and make informed decisions."

He clicked to the next slide, which displayed the phrase: "Decision Making."

"The final step in policy analysis is decision-making," Dr. Hayes said. "Policymakers must choose the policy option that best aligns with their goals, values, and priorities. This often involves negotiation, compromise, and consensus-building among stakeholders."

As the lecture continued, Dr. Hayes guided his students through the complexities of policy analysis and decision-making. From problem definition to option analysis and final decision-making, policymakers navigated a complex landscape of competing interests and values to craft policies that served the public interest.

"As you continue your studies," Dr. Hayes concluded, "consider the challenges and opportunities inherent in policy analysis and decision-making, and the role they play in shaping the policy landscape."

The students left the lecture hall, their minds buzzing with newfound insights into the intricacies of policy analysis and decision-making. Dr. Hayes watched them go, feeling a sense of satisfaction at having deepened their understanding of this critical aspect of public administration.

Stakeholder Engagement and Public Participation

Dr. Robert Hayes stepped into the classroom, prepared to explore the essential role of stakeholder engagement and public participation in the policy-making process. This aspect of policy development was crucial for ensuring transparency, accountability, and legitimacy in governance.

"Good morning, class," Dr. Hayes greeted, his voice resonating with energy. "Today, we delve into the importance of stakeholder engagement and public participation in the policy-making process, examining how involving diverse stakeholders and the public enhances the quality and legitimacy of policies."

He clicked to the first slide, displaying the title: "Stakeholder Engagement and Public Participation."

"Stakeholder engagement," Dr. Hayes began, "involves actively involving individuals, groups, and organizations that have a vested interest in or are affected by a particular policy issue. It ensures that a wide range of perspectives and expertise are considered in the decision-making process."

As he spoke, images of policymakers meeting with community members, advocacy groups, and industry representatives filled the screen, illustrating the diverse array of stakeholders involved in policy discussions.

"The first step in stakeholder engagement is identifying key stakeholders," Dr. Hayes continued. "These may include government agencies, non-profit organizations, businesses, community groups, and individuals directly impacted by the policy under consideration."

A hand shot up from a student named Emily. "How do policymakers engage stakeholders effectively?"

"Policymakers can engage stakeholders through various methods, including public hearings, town hall meetings, focus groups, and advisory committees," Dr. Hayes replied. "They may also use online platforms, surveys, and consultations to solicit input from a broader audience. Effective communication, transparency, and inclusivity are essential for building trust and fostering meaningful engagement."

He clicked to the next slide, which read: "Public Participation."

"Public participation," Dr. Hayes explained, "refers to the active involvement of citizens in the policy-making process. It empowers individuals to contribute their perspectives, experiences, and expertise to inform policy decisions that affect their lives."

A student named Marcus raised his hand. "Why is public participation important in policymaking?"

"Public participation enhances the legitimacy, accountability, and effectiveness of policies," Dr. Hayes replied. "By involving citizens in the decision-making process, policymakers ensure that policies reflect the needs, values, and priorities of the public they serve. Public participation also fosters civic engagement, trust in government, and social cohesion."

He clicked to the next slide, which displayed the phrase: "Benefits of Stakeholder Engagement and Public Participation."

"The benefits of stakeholder engagement and public participation are numerous," Dr. Hayes said. "They lead to more informed and robust policy decisions, increased public trust and satisfaction, and improved implementation and outcomes. By involving stakeholders and the public in the policy-making process, policymakers can create policies that better reflect the diverse needs and interests of society."

As the lecture continued, Dr. Hayes guided his students through examples of successful stakeholder engagement and public participation initiatives, highlighting their impact on policy development and implementation.

"As you continue your studies," Dr. Hayes concluded, "consider the importance of stakeholder engagement and public participation in promoting inclusive, transparent, and effective governance."

The students left the lecture hall, inspired by the possibilities of stakeholder engagement and public participation in shaping the policies that impact their communities. Dr. Hayes watched them go, feeling a sense of optimism for the future of participatory democracy.

Public Expenditure Management

Dr. Robert Hayes stood before his students, ready to delve into the critical aspect of public expenditure management in the policy-making process. This topic was essential for understanding how governments allocate resources to fund public policies and programs, ensuring efficient and effective use of taxpayer money.

"Good morning, class," Dr. Hayes greeted, his voice projecting authority. "Today, we explore the intricacies of public expenditure management, examining how governments budget, allocate, and manage financial resources to support their policy objectives."

He clicked to the first slide, displaying the title: "Public Expenditure Management."

"Public expenditure management," Dr. Hayes began, "refers to the process by which governments plan, allocate, and control spending to achieve their policy goals while ensuring fiscal sustainability and accountability."

As he spoke, images of budget documents, financial reports, and government officials overseeing expenditure filled the screen, illustrating the complexity of public financial management.

"The first step in public expenditure management is budget formulation," Dr. Hayes continued. "During this stage, governments assess their revenue sources, set expenditure priorities, and allocate funds to different programs and activities."

A hand shot up from a student named Emily. "How do governments prioritize spending in the budget formulation process?"

"Governments prioritize spending based on their policy objectives, economic conditions, and revenue constraints," Dr. Hayes replied. "They may use various budgeting techniques, such as zero-based budgeting or performance-based budgeting, to allocate resources to areas with the greatest need or potential impact."

He clicked to the next slide, which read: "Budget Execution."

"The next stage in public expenditure management is budget execution," Dr. Hayes explained. "During this stage, governments implement their budget plans by authorizing expenditures, monitoring spending, and ensuring compliance with budgetary regulations."

A student named Marcus raised his hand. "How do governments ensure transparency and accountability in budget execution?"

"Governments ensure transparency and accountability through rigorous financial reporting, internal controls, and independent audits," Dr. Hayes replied. "They also engage stakeholders and the public in the budget process to foster accountability and trust in government spending."

He clicked to the next slide, which displayed the phrase:

"Budget Monitoring and Evaluation."

"The final stage in public expenditure management is budget monitoring and evaluation," Dr. Hayes said. "During this stage, governments assess the performance and impact of their spending decisions, identifying areas for improvement and making adjustments as needed."

As the lecture continued, Dr. Hayes guided his students through examples of effective public expenditure management practices, highlighting the importance of sound financial management in achieving policy objectives and fostering public trust.

"As you continue your studies," Dr. Hayes concluded, "consider the role of public expenditure management in promoting fiscal responsibility, transparency, and accountability in government."

The students left the lecture hall, their minds buzzing with newfound insights into the complexities of public expenditure management. Dr. Hayes watched them go, feeling a sense of satisfaction at having deepened their understanding of this critical aspect of public administration.

Financial Accountability and Transparency

Dr. Robert Hayes entered the classroom with purpose, ready to explore the essential principles of financial accountability and transparency in the policy-making process. This aspect of public expenditure management was crucial for ensuring integrity and trust in government financial practices.

"Good morning, class," Dr. Hayes greeted, his voice resonating with gravitas. "Today, we delve into the principles of financial accountability and transparency, examining how governments uphold these principles to safeguard public funds and foster trust in their financial management."

He clicked to the first slide, displaying the title: "Financial Accountability and Transparency."

"Financial accountability," Dr. Hayes began, "refers to the obligation of governments to use public funds responsibly, efficiently, and in accordance with established laws and regulations."

As he spoke, images of financial reports, audit findings, and government officials overseeing financial processes filled the screen, illustrating the importance of accountability in public financial management.

"The first principle of financial accountability is internal controls," Dr. Hayes continued. "Governments establish internal controls to safeguard assets, prevent fraud and misuse of funds, and ensure compliance with financial regulations."

A hand shot up from a student named Emily. "How do governments ensure the effectiveness of internal controls?"

"Governments ensure the effectiveness of internal controls through regular monitoring, evaluation, and enforcement," Dr. Hayes replied. "They may conduct internal audits, implement segregation of duties, and provide training to staff to enhance their awareness of financial responsibilities."

He clicked to the next slide, which read: "Financial Transparency."

"The second principle of financial accountability is transparency," Dr. Hayes explained. "Transparency refers to the openness and accessibility of government financial information to the public."

A student named Marcus raised his hand. "Why is financial transparency important?"

"Financial transparency is important for several reasons," Dr. Hayes replied. "It allows citizens to hold government officials accountable for their use of public funds, promotes public trust and confidence in government financial management, and facilitates informed decision-making by stakeholders."

He clicked to the next slide, which displayed the phrase: "Promoting Financial Accountability and Transparency."

"Governments promote financial accountability and transparency through various mechanisms," Dr. Hayes said. "These may include publishing budget documents, financial statements, and audit reports online, conducting public hearings on budget matters, and engaging with stakeholders to solicit feedback on financial management practices."

As the lecture continued, Dr. Hayes guided his students through examples of governments that had successfully implemented measures to enhance financial accountability and transparency, highlighting their impact on governance and public trust.

"As you continue your studies," Dr. Hayes concluded, "consider the importance of financial accountability and transparency in promoting good governance and ensuring the responsible use of public funds."

The students left the lecture hall, inspired by the principles of financial accountability and transparency in government. Dr. Hayes watched them go, feeling a sense of optimism for the future of transparent and accountable governance.

Policy Implementation and Evaluation

Dr. Robert Hayes stood before his students, prepared to explore the critical stages of policy implementation and evaluation in the policy-making process. This aspect of policy development was essential for understanding how policies are put into action and assessed for their effectiveness.

"Good morning, class," Dr. Hayes greeted, his voice brimming with enthusiasm. "Today, we delve into the dynamic processes of policy implementation and evaluation, examining how governments translate policy goals into tangible actions and assess the impact of their policies on society."

He clicked to the first slide, displaying the title: "Policy Implementation and Evaluation."

"Policy implementation," Dr. Hayes began, "is the process by which governments put policy decisions into practice, allocating resources, establishing procedures, and delivering services to achieve policy objectives."

As he spoke, images of government officials working with stakeholders, implementing programs, and monitoring progress filled the screen, illustrating the complexity of policy implementation.

"The first step in policy implementation is translating policy goals into actionable plans," Dr. Hayes continued. "This involves defining clear objectives, assigning responsibilities, and allocating resources to support the implementation process."

A hand shot up from a student named Emily. "How do governments ensure effective implementation of policies?"

"Effective implementation requires coordination, communication, and collaboration among government agencies, stakeholders, and the public," Dr. Hayes replied. "Governments may use tools such as project management techniques, performance monitoring systems, and capacity-building initiatives to facilitate implementation and address challenges as they arise."

He clicked to the next slide, which read: "Policy Evaluation."

"The next stage in the policy-making process is policy evaluation," Dr. Hayes explained. "Policy evaluation involves assessing the impact and outcomes of policies to determine their effectiveness, efficiency, and relevance."

A student named Marcus raised his hand. "How do governments evaluate the impact of their policies?"

"Governments use various methods and techniques to evaluate policy impact," Dr. Hayes replied. "These may include quantitative data analysis, surveys, case studies, and stakeholder consultations. By measuring outcomes against predetermined objectives, governments can assess whether their policies are achieving the desired results and make adjustments as needed."

He clicked to the next slide, which displayed the phrase: "Continuous Improvement."

"The goal of policy evaluation is not only to assess past performance but also to inform future decision-making and improve policy outcomes," Dr. Hayes said. "By identifying strengths, weaknesses, and areas for improvement, governments can refine their policies, allocate resources more effectively, and better serve the needs of society."

As the lecture continued, Dr. Hayes guided his students through examples of policy implementation and evaluation processes, highlighting the importance of continuous learning and adaptation in governance.

"As you continue your studies," Dr. Hayes concluded,

"consider the complexities of policy implementation and evaluation and the role they play in shaping effective and responsive governance."

The students left the lecture hall, their minds buzzing with newfound insights into the dynamic processes of policy implementation and evaluation. Dr. Hayes watched them go, feeling a sense of satisfaction at having deepened their understanding of this critical aspect of public administration.

Case Studies in Public Policy

Dr. Robert Hayes stood before his students, eager to delve into real-world examples of public policies in action. Case studies offered a practical lens through which students could explore the complexities and challenges of policy development, implementation, and evaluation.

"Good morning, class," Dr. Hayes greeted, his voice filled with anticipation. "Today, we embark on a journey through case studies in public policy, examining real-world examples of policies that have shaped governance and impacted society."

He clicked to the first slide, displaying the title: "Case Studies in Public Policy."

"Case studies," Dr. Hayes began, "offer valuable insights into the practical application of theoretical concepts and principles discussed in this course. By analyzing actual policy initiatives, we can better understand the factors that influence policy outcomes and the lessons learned from both successes and failures."

As he spoke, images of diverse policy initiatives, from healthcare reforms to environmental regulations, filled the screen, illustrating the breadth and depth of public policy.

"Our first case study," Dr. Hayes continued, "examines the Affordable Care Act (ACA) in the United States. Enacted in 2010, the ACA aimed to expand access to healthcare coverage, improve quality of care, and reduce healthcare costs."

A hand shot up from a student named Emily. "What were some of the key challenges in implementing the ACA?"

"Implementing the ACA faced numerous challenges, including political opposition, technical complexities, and resistance from stakeholders," Dr. Hayes replied. "States had to navigate issues such as Medicaid expansion, insurance market reforms, and the rollout of healthcare exchanges, leading to varied experiences and outcomes across the country."

He clicked to the next slide, which read: "Lessons Learned."

"From the ACA case study, we can glean several lessons," Dr. Hayes explained. "The importance of stakeholder engagement, the need for effective communication, and the challenges of navigating political dynamics in policymaking. While the ACA expanded healthcare coverage for millions of Americans, it also highlighted the complexities of healthcare reform and the ongoing debate over the role of government in healthcare."

A student named Marcus raised his hand. "What other case studies will we explore?"

"We will explore a range of case studies across different policy areas, including education, environmental protection, economic development, and social welfare," Dr. Hayes replied. "Each case study offers unique insights into the complexities of policy-making, implementation, and evaluation, providing valuable lessons for future policymakers and public administrators."

He clicked to the next slide, which displayed the phrase: "Analyzing Policy Outcomes."

"As we analyze these case studies," Dr. Hayes said, "we will consider not only the intended outcomes of policies but also their unintended consequences, distributional impacts, and equity considerations. By examining policies from multiple perspectives, we can gain a more comprehensive understanding of their effects on society."

As the lecture continued, Dr. Hayes guided his students through a series of case studies, encouraging them to critically analyze each example and draw connections to theoretical concepts discussed in class.

"As you study these case studies," Dr. Hayes concluded, "consider the complexities and nuances of policy-making in the real world and the importance of evidence-based decision-making in shaping effective governance."

The students left the lecture hall, eager to dive into the world of public policy through case studies. Dr. Hayes watched them go, feeling a sense of excitement at the opportunities for learning and discovery that lay ahead.

5

Chapter 5: Public Budgeting and Financial Management

Principles of Public Budgeting

D r. Robert Hayes strode into the classroom with purpose, ready to unveil the fundamental principles that underpin public budgeting and financial management. This chapter was crucial for understanding how governments allocate resources to meet the needs of society while maintaining fiscal responsibility.

"Good morning, class," Dr. Hayes greeted, his voice commanding attention. "Today, we embark on a journey through the principles of public budgeting, exploring the core concepts that guide governments in allocating financial resources to support their policy objectives."

He clicked to the first slide, displaying the title: "Principles of Public Budgeting."

"Public budgeting," Dr. Hayes began, "is the process by which governments allocate resources to fund public programs and services, prioritize spending, and manage financial resources to achieve policy goals."

As he spoke, images of budget documents, revenue charts, and government officials deliberating over financial plans filled the screen, illustrating the intricacies of public budgeting.

"The first principle of public budgeting is fiscal responsibility," Dr. Hayes continued. "Governments must balance their budgets, avoid deficit spending, and ensure that expenditures do not exceed revenues over the long term."

A hand shot up from a student named Emily. "How do governments achieve fiscal responsibility in budgeting?"

"Governments achieve fiscal responsibility through prudent financial management practices, such as revenue forecasting, expenditure control, and debt management," Dr. Hayes replied. "They may also establish fiscal rules, such as balanced budget requirements or debt ceilings, to enforce fiscal discipline and promote sustainability."

He clicked to the next slide, which read: "Budget Transparency."

"The second principle of public budgeting is transparency," Dr. Hayes explained. "Transparency refers to the openness and accessibility of budget information to the public, ensuring accountability and promoting trust in government financial management."

A student named Marcus raised his hand. "Why is budget transparency important?"

"Budget transparency is essential for democratic governance," Dr. Hayes replied. "It allows citizens to understand how public funds are raised and spent, hold government officials accountable for their financial decisions, and participate in the budget process."

He clicked to the next slide, which displayed the phrase: "Allocating Resources Effectively."

"The third principle of public budgeting is allocating resources effectively," Dr. Hayes said. "Governments must prioritize spending to address the most pressing needs of society, maximize the impact of limited resources, and achieve the greatest return on investment."

As the lecture continued, Dr. Hayes guided his students through the remaining principles of public budgeting, illustrating each concept with real-world examples and practical insights.

"As you study the principles of public budgeting," Dr. Hayes concluded, "consider the challenges and opportunities inherent in allocating and managing public resources and the role they play in shaping effective governance."

The students left the lecture hall, their minds buzzing with newfound insights into the principles of public budgeting. Dr. Hayes watched them go, feeling a sense of satisfaction at having laid the foundation for their understanding of this critical aspect of public administration.

Budget Preparation and Approval Process

Dr. Robert Hayes stood before his students, ready to unravel the intricate process of budget preparation and approval. This stage of public budgeting was crucial for understanding how governments develop and finalize their financial plans to allocate resources effectively.

"Good morning, class," Dr. Hayes greeted, his voice filled with anticipation. "Today, we journey through the labyrinth of budget preparation and approval, exploring the steps involved in crafting and ratifying government budgets."

He clicked to the first slide, displaying the title: "Budget Preparation and Approval Process."

"Budget preparation," Dr. Hayes began, "is the process by which governments develop their financial plans, projecting revenues, estimating expenditures, and prioritizing spending to achieve policy objectives."

As he spoke, images of government officials analyzing data, drafting budget proposals, and consulting with stakeholders filled the screen, illustrating the complexity of budget preparation.

"The first step in budget preparation is revenue forecasting," Dr. Hayes continued. "Governments must estimate the amount of revenue they expect to collect from taxes, fees, and other sources to fund their expenditures."

A hand shot up from a student named Emily. "How do governments forecast revenues accurately?"

"Revenue forecasting requires a combination of economic analysis, historical data, and expert judgment," Dr. Hayes replied. "Governments may consult with economists, financial analysts, and revenue agencies to develop realistic revenue projections based on economic trends and policy changes."

He clicked to the next slide, which read: "Expenditure Estimation."

"The next step in budget preparation is estimating expenditures," Dr. Hayes explained. "Governments must project the cost of providing public services, funding programs, and maintaining infrastructure to determine how resources will be allocated."

A student named Marcus raised his hand. "How do governments prioritize spending during budget preparation?"

"Governments prioritize spending based on their policy objectives, strategic priorities, and available resources," Dr. Hayes replied. "They may use budgetary tools, such as performance-based budgeting or program evaluation, to assess the effectiveness and efficiency of programs and allocate resources to areas with the greatest need or impact."

He clicked to the next slide, which displayed the phrase: "Budget Approval Process."

"The final stage in budget preparation is the approval process," Dr. Hayes said. "Once the budget proposal is drafted, it must be reviewed, revised, and approved by the appropriate legislative body, such as a city council or parliament."

As the lecture continued, Dr. Hayes guided his students through examples of budget preparation and approval processes at the local, state, and national levels, highlighting the role of political dynamics, stakeholder interests, and fiscal constraints in shaping budget outcomes.

"As you study the budget preparation and approval process," Dr. Hayes concluded, "consider the complexities and challenges inherent in crafting government budgets and the importance of transparency, accountability, and public participation in ensuring effective fiscal management."

The students left the lecture hall, their minds buzzing with newfound insights into the intricacies of budget preparation and approval. Dr. Hayes watched them go, feeling a sense of satisfaction at having demystified this critical aspect of public administration.

Revenue Generation and Taxation

Dr. Robert Hayes stepped into the classroom, ready to explore the mechanisms of revenue generation and taxation in public budgeting. This aspect of financial management was crucial for understanding how governments fund their operations and services.

"Good morning, class," Dr. Hayes greeted, his voice projecting authority. "Today, we delve into the intricacies of revenue generation and taxation, examining how governments raise the funds needed to finance public programs and services."

He clicked to the first slide, displaying the title: "Revenue Generation and Taxation."

"Revenue generation," Dr. Hayes began, "is the process by which governments collect funds to support their activities and fulfill their obligations to society."

As he spoke, images of tax forms, revenue streams, and government agencies responsible for collecting taxes filled the screen, illustrating the diverse sources of government revenue.

"The primary source of government revenue is taxation," Dr. Hayes continued. "Taxes are levied on individuals, businesses, and other entities to generate income for the government."

A hand shot up from a student named Emily. "What are the different types of taxes?"

"There are various types of taxes, including income taxes, sales taxes, property taxes, and corporate taxes," Dr. Hayes replied. "Each type of tax serves a different purpose and may be levied at different rates depending on the jurisdiction."

He clicked to the next slide, which read: "Principles of Taxation."

"The principles of taxation guide governments in designing tax policies that are equitable, efficient, and effective," Dr. Hayes explained. "These principles include fairness, simplicity, efficiency, and transparency."

A student named Marcus raised his hand. "How do governments ensure fairness in taxation?"

"Governments strive to achieve fairness in taxation by implementing progressive, proportional, or regressive tax systems," Dr. Hayes replied. "Progressive taxes impose higher rates on individuals with higher incomes, while proportional taxes apply the same rate to all taxpayers, and regressive taxes impose higher rates on lower-income individuals."

He clicked to the next slide, which displayed the phrase: "Challenges of Taxation."

"Despite its importance, taxation presents several challenges for governments," Dr. Hayes said. "These may include tax evasion, tax avoidance, administrative complexities, and economic distortions. Governments must address these challenges to ensure the effectiveness and fairness of their tax systems."

As the lecture continued, Dr. Hayes guided his students through examples of tax policies and their implications for government revenue and fiscal policy, highlighting the trade-offs and considerations involved in tax design.

"As you study revenue generation and taxation," Dr. Hayes concluded, "consider the role of taxation in funding government activities and the challenges and opportunities inherent in designing equitable and efficient tax systems."

The students left the lecture hall, their minds buzzing with newfound insights into the complexities of revenue generation and taxation. Dr. Hayes watched them go, feeling a sense of satisfaction at having deepened their understanding of this critical aspect of public administration.

Public Expenditure Management

Dr. Robert Hayes entered the classroom, prepared to dissect the critical process of public expenditure management. This stage of financial management was essential for understanding how governments allocate and manage funds to deliver public services effectively.

"Good morning, class," Dr. Hayes greeted, his voice filled with purpose. "Today, we explore the realm of public expenditure management, examining how governments allocate resources and oversee spending to achieve policy objectives."

He clicked to the first slide, displaying the title: "Public Expenditure Management."

"Public expenditure management," Dr. Hayes began, "encompasses the processes by which governments plan, allocate, and control spending to achieve their policy goals while ensuring fiscal responsibility."

As he spoke, images of government agencies, budget reports, and expenditure tracking systems filled the screen, illustrating the complexity of managing public funds.

"The first step in public expenditure management is budget allocation," Dr. Hayes continued. "Governments allocate funds to different programs, agencies, and initiatives based on their policy priorities and strategic objectives."

A hand shot up from a student named Emily. "How do governments ensure that funds are allocated effectively?"

"Effective budget allocation requires careful planning, analysis, and prioritization," Dr. Hayes replied. "Governments may use budgetary tools such as performance-based budgeting, cost-benefit analysis, and outcome-based budgeting to allocate resources to areas with the greatest impact and return on investment."

He clicked to the next slide, which read: "Expenditure Monitoring and Control."

"The next stage in public expenditure management is expenditure monitoring and control," Dr. Hayes explained. "Governments must monitor spending to ensure that funds are used as intended and control expenditures to prevent waste, fraud, and abuse."

A student named Marcus raised his hand. "How do governments monitor and control expenditures?"

"Governments monitor expenditures through financial reporting, internal audits, and performance evaluations," Dr. Hayes replied. "They may establish internal controls, such as procurement regulations and spending limits, to prevent unauthorized spending and ensure compliance with budgetary requirements."

He clicked to the next slide, which displayed the phrase: "Ensuring Accountability and Transparency."

"The final aspect of public expenditure management is ensuring accountability and transparency," Dr. Hayes said. "Governments must be accountable to citizens for how public funds are used and transparently communicate financial information to the public."

As the lecture continued, Dr. Hayes guided his students through examples of effective public expenditure management practices, highlighting the importance of accountability, transparency, and fiscal responsibility in governance.

"As you study public expenditure management," Dr. Hayes

concluded, "consider the challenges and opportunities inherent in allocating and overseeing public funds and the role they play in achieving policy objectives and fostering public trust."

The students left the lecture hall, their minds buzzing with newfound insights into the complexities of public expenditure management. Dr. Hayes watched them go, feeling a sense of satisfaction at having illuminated this critical aspect of public administration.

Financial Accountability and Transparency

Dr. Robert Hayes entered the classroom, prepared to explore the crucial principles of financial accountability and transparency in public budgeting. This aspect of financial management was essential for ensuring integrity and trust in government fiscal practices.

"Good morning, class," Dr. Hayes greeted, his voice resonating with authority. "Today, we delve into the principles of financial accountability and transparency, examining how governments uphold these principles to safeguard public funds and foster trust in their financial management."

He clicked to the first slide, displaying the title: "Financial Accountability and Transparency."

"Financial accountability," Dr. Hayes began, "refers to the obligation of governments to use public funds responsibly, efficiently, and in accordance with established laws and regulations."

As he spoke, images of financial reports, audit findings, and government officials overseeing financial processes filled the screen, illustrating the importance of accountability in public financial management.

"The first principle of financial accountability is internal controls," Dr. Hayes continued. "Governments establish internal controls to safeguard assets, prevent fraud and misuse of funds, and ensure compliance with financial regulations."

A hand shot up from a student named Emily. "How do governments ensure the effectiveness of internal controls?"

"Governments ensure the effectiveness of internal controls through regular monitoring, evaluation, and enforcement," Dr. Hayes replied. "They may conduct internal audits, implement segregation of duties, and provide training to staff to enhance their awareness of financial responsibilities."

He clicked to the next slide, which read: "Financial Transparency."

"The second principle of financial accountability is transparency," Dr. Hayes explained. "Transparency refers to the openness and accessibility of government financial information to the public."

A student named Marcus raised his hand. "Why is financial transparency important?"

"Financial transparency is important for several reasons," Dr. Hayes replied. "It allows citizens to hold government officials accountable for their use of public funds, promotes public trust and confidence in government financial management, and facilitates informed decision-making by stakeholders."

He clicked to the next slide, which displayed the phrase: "Promoting Financial Accountability and Transparency."

"Governments promote financial accountability and transparency through various mechanisms," Dr. Hayes said. "These may include publishing budget documents, financial statements, and audit reports online, conducting public hearings on budget matters, and engaging with stakeholders to solicit feedback on financial management practices."

As the lecture continued, Dr. Hayes guided his students through examples of governments that had successfully implemented measures to enhance financial accountability and transparency, highlighting their impact on governance and public trust.

"As you continue your studies," Dr. Hayes concluded, "consider the importance of financial accountability and transparency in promoting good governance and ensuring the responsible use of public funds."

The students left the lecture hall, inspired by the principles of financial accountability and transparency in government. Dr. Hayes watched them go, feeling a sense of optimism for the future of transparent and accountable governance.

Case Studies in Public Finance

Dr. Robert Hayes stood before his students, eager to dive into real-world examples of public finance in action. Case studies offered a practical lens through which students could explore the complexities and challenges of budgeting, revenue generation, expenditure management, and financial accountability.

"Good morning, class," Dr. Hayes greeted, his voice brimming with enthusiasm. "Today, we embark on a journey through case studies in public finance, examining how governments navigate fiscal challenges, allocate resources, and manage finances to meet the needs of society."

He clicked to the first slide, displaying the title: "Case Studies in Public Finance."

"Case studies," Dr. Hayes began, "offer valuable insights into the practical application of concepts and principles discussed in this course. By analyzing actual financial situations and decisions, we can better understand the dynamics of public finance and draw lessons for effective fiscal management."

As he spoke, images of budget crises, revenue shortfalls, infrastructure projects, and public service delivery filled the screen, illustrating the breadth and depth of public finance challenges.

"Our first case study," Dr. Hayes continued, "examines the financial crisis faced by the city of Detroit in 2013. Plagued by declining population, economic decline, and unsustainable pension obligations, Detroit filed for bankruptcy, becoming the largest municipal bankruptcy in U.S. history."

A hand shot up from a student named Emily. "What were some of the key factors contributing to Detroit's financial crisis?"

"The financial crisis in Detroit was caused by a combination of long-term structural challenges, including population decline, loss of tax revenue, and unsustainable pension costs," Dr. Hayes replied. "Poor financial management practices, ineffective budgeting, and limited economic diversification exacerbated the city's fiscal woes."

He clicked to the next slide, which read: "Lessons Learned."

"From the Detroit case study, we can glean several lessons," Dr. Hayes explained. "The importance of proactive fiscal management, long-term planning, and addressing structural challenges before they escalate into crises. Detroit's experience underscores the need for governments to prioritize financial sustainability and resilience in their fiscal policies."

A student named Marcus raised his hand. "What other case studies will we explore?"

"We will explore a range of case studies across different

sectors and jurisdictions," Dr. Hayes replied. "From successful infrastructure projects to innovative revenue generation initiatives, each case study offers unique insights into the complexities of public finance and the strategies governments employ to address fiscal challenges."

He clicked to the next slide, which displayed the phrase: "Applying Lessons to Practice."

"As we analyze these case studies," Dr. Hayes said, "we will consider how the lessons learned can be applied to real-world situations, informing our understanding of effective fiscal management and guiding future decision-making by policymakers and public administrators."

As the lecture continued, Dr. Hayes guided his students through a series of case studies, encouraging them to critically analyze each example and draw connections to the principles and practices of public finance discussed in class.

"As you study these case studies," Dr. Hayes concluded, "consider the complexities and nuances of public finance and the importance of evidence-based decision-making in achieving fiscal sustainability and advancing public welfare."

The students left the lecture hall, their minds buzzing with newfound insights into the challenges and opportunities of public finance. Dr. Hayes watched them go, feeling a sense of satisfaction at having illuminated the practical realities of fiscal management in government.

6

Chapter 6: Human Resource Management in Public Administration

Recruitment and Selection Processes

Dr. Robert Hayes entered the classroom, ready to unravel the complexities of human resource management in public administration. This chapter was crucial for understanding how governments attract, select, and retain talented individuals to fulfill their missions effectively.

"Good morning, class," Dr. Hayes greeted, his voice resonating with authority. "Today, we delve into the realm of human resource management in public administration, focusing on the recruitment and selection processes that shape the workforce of government organizations."

He clicked to the first slide, displaying the title: "Recruitment and Selection Processes."

"Recruitment and selection," Dr. Hayes began, "are critical components of human resource management, as they determine the quality and composition of the government workforce."

As he spoke, images of job postings, recruitment fairs, and selection panels filled the screen, illustrating the various stages of the recruitment and selection process.

"The first stage in human resource management is recruitment," Dr. Hayes continued. "Recruitment involves attracting qualified candidates to apply for positions within the government organization."

A hand shot up from a student named Emily. "How do governments attract candidates to public service?"

"Governments use various strategies to attract candidates to public service, including targeted advertising, recruitment events, and partnerships with educational institutions," Dr. Hayes replied. "They may also emphasize the unique opportunities for career development, job security, and public service impact that government positions offer."

He clicked to the next slide, which read: "Selection Processes."

"The next stage in human resource management is the selection process," Dr. Hayes explained. "Selection involves evaluating candidates to determine their suitability for specific positions based on their qualifications, skills, and abilities."

A student named Marcus raised his hand. "What are some common selection methods used in public administration?"

"Common selection methods in public administration include application screening, interviews, assessment tests, and reference checks," Dr. Hayes replied. "These methods help ensure that candidates possess the necessary competencies and attributes to perform effectively in their roles."

He clicked to the next slide, which displayed the phrase: "Ensuring Fairness and Diversity."

"Fairness and diversity are essential considerations in recruitment and selection," Dr. Hayes said. "Governments must strive to create inclusive recruitment processes that attract a diverse pool of candidates and ensure equal opportunities for all applicants."

As the lecture continued, Dr. Hayes guided his students through examples of effective recruitment and selection practices in public administration, highlighting the importance of fairness, transparency, and meritocracy in building a skilled and diverse workforce.

"As you study recruitment and selection processes," Dr. Hayes concluded, "consider the role they play in shaping the composition and effectiveness of government organizations and the opportunities they present for advancing diversity, equity, and inclusion."

The students left the lecture hall, inspired by the principles of recruitment and selection in public administration. Dr. Hayes watched them go, feeling a sense of optimism for the future of talent management in government.

Training and Professional Development

Dr. Robert Hayes, with a fervent zeal for professional growth, stepped into the classroom, ready to enlighten his students on the vital aspects of training and professional development in public administration. This segment was crucial for understanding how governments nurture talent, enhance skills, and foster continuous improvement among their workforce.

"Good morning, class," Dr. Hayes greeted, his voice pulsating with enthusiasm. "Today, we delve into the realm of training and professional development in public administration, exploring how governments invest in their employees' growth and proficiency."

He clicked to the first slide, unveiling the title: "Training and Professional Development."

"Training and professional development," Dr. Hayes began, "are essential components of human resource management, as they enable employees to acquire new skills, enhance existing competencies, and adapt to evolving job requirements."

As he spoke, images of workshops, seminars, online courses, and mentorship programs filled the screen, depicting the myriad opportunities available for employee growth and development.

"The first aspect of training and professional development is skills enhancement," Dr. Hayes continued. "Governments provide training programs to equip employees with the knowledge and skills needed to perform their jobs effectively."

A hand shot up from a student named Emily. "How do governments design training programs to meet employees' needs?"

"Governments design training programs based on job requirements, performance evaluations, and employee feedback," Dr. Hayes replied. "They may offer a mix of classroom training, on-the-job learning, and e-learning opportunities to accommodate different learning styles and preferences."

He clicked to the next slide, which read: "Career Advancement."

"The next aspect of training and professional development is career advancement," Dr. Hayes explained. "Governments provide opportunities for employees to advance their careers through promotions, lateral moves, and leadership development programs."

A student named Marcus raised his hand. "How do governments support leadership development?"

"Governments support leadership development through mentorship programs, executive coaching, and leadership training initiatives," Dr. Hayes replied. "They identify high-potential employees and provide them with opportunities to enhance their leadership skills and prepare for future leadership roles."

He clicked to the next slide, which displayed the phrase: "Fostering a Learning Culture."

"Fostering a learning culture is essential for creating an environment where employees feel encouraged to pursue continuous learning and development," Dr. Hayes said. "Governments promote a learning culture through recognition of learning achievements, incentives for professional development, and support for knowledge sharing and collaboration."

As the lecture continued, Dr. Hayes guided his students through examples of successful training and professional development programs in public administration, highlighting their impact on employee engagement, job satisfaction, and organizational performance.

"As you explore training and professional development," Dr. Hayes concluded, "consider the role they play in enhancing employee capabilities, driving organizational success, and fostering a culture of innovation and excellence in public administration."

The students left the lecture hall, inspired by the possibilities of personal and professional growth in public service. Dr. Hayes watched them go, feeling a sense of fulfillment at having ignited their passion for continuous learning and development.

Performance Management Systems

Dr. Robert Hayes strode into the classroom with an air of purpose, ready to delve into the intricacies of performance management systems in public administration. This segment was pivotal for understanding how governments assess, motivate, and enhance employee performance to achieve organizational goals.

"Good morning, class," Dr. Hayes greeted, his voice exuding authority. "Today, we explore the realm of performance management systems in public administration, examining how governments evaluate employee performance and foster a culture of accountability and excellence."

He clicked to the first slide, revealing the title: "Performance Management Systems."

"Performance management systems," Dr. Hayes began, "are essential tools for aligning individual performance with organizational objectives, providing feedback, and facilitating continuous improvement."

As he spoke, images of performance evaluations, goal-setting sessions, and performance improvement plans filled the screen, illustrating the multifaceted nature of performance management.

"The first aspect of performance management is goal setting," Dr. Hayes continued. "Governments establish clear and measurable goals for employees, aligning them with organizational priorities and individual responsibilities."

A hand shot up from a student named Emily. "How do governments ensure that goals are meaningful and achievable?"

"Governments ensure meaningful and achievable goals through collaboration between managers and employees," Dr. Hayes replied. "They engage in dialogue to clarify expectations, set realistic targets, and ensure that goals are aligned with the organization's mission and strategic objectives."

He clicked to the next slide, which read: "Performance Evaluation."

"The next aspect of performance management is performance evaluation," Dr. Hayes explained. "Governments assess employee performance against established goals and competencies, providing feedback and identifying areas for improvement."

A student named Marcus raised his hand. "How do governments conduct performance evaluations fairly and objectively?"

"Governments conduct fair and objective performance evaluations through standardized criteria, multiple sources of feedback, and regular performance discussions," Dr. Hayes replied. "They may use performance rating scales, 360-degree feedback, and self-assessment tools to gather comprehensive insights into employee performance."

He clicked to the next slide, which displayed the phrase: "Performance Improvement."

"The final aspect of performance management is performance improvement," Dr. Hayes said. "Governments provide support and resources to help employees enhance their performance, address skill gaps, and achieve their full potential."

As the lecture continued, Dr. Hayes guided his students through examples of performance management systems in public administration, highlighting best practices and innovative approaches to performance evaluation and improvement.

"As you explore performance management systems," Dr. Hayes concluded, "consider their role in driving employee engagement, motivation, and organizational success, and the opportunities they present for continuous learning and development."

The students left the lecture hall, inspired by the potential of performance management to unleash individual and organizational excellence. Dr. Hayes watched them go, feeling a sense of pride at having illuminated the path to performance excellence in public administration.

Labor Relations and Collective Bargaining

Dr. Robert Hayes entered the classroom with a sense of anticipation, prepared to navigate the complexities of labor relations and collective bargaining in public administration. This aspect of human resource management was crucial for understanding how governments engage with employee unions to negotiate working conditions, wages, and benefits.

"Good morning, class," Dr. Hayes greeted, his voice projecting confidence. "Today, we embark on a journey into the realm of labor relations and collective bargaining, exploring the dynamics of employee-employer interactions and the negotiation processes that shape working conditions in the public sector."

He clicked to the first slide, unveiling the title: "Labor Relations and Collective Bargaining."

"Labor relations," Dr. Hayes began, "refer to the interactions between management and labor unions representing employees in the workplace. Collective bargaining is the process by which these parties negotiate agreements on wages, benefits, and working conditions."

As he spoke, images of labor strikes, negotiation tables, and union representatives filled the screen, illustrating the power dynamics and negotiations involved in labor relations.

"The first aspect of labor relations is unionization," Dr. Hayes continued. "Employees may choose to unionize to collectively bargain for better wages, benefits, and working conditions."

A hand shot up from a student named Emily. "How do unions impact the public sector?"

"Unions can have a significant impact on the public sector by advocating for the interests of employees, influencing labor policies, and shaping workplace practices," Dr. Hayes replied. "They negotiate collective bargaining agreements with government employers to establish terms and conditions of employment for unionized employees."

He clicked to the next slide, which read: "Collective Bargaining Process."

"The collective bargaining process typically involves several stages," Dr. Hayes explained. "These may include preparation, negotiation, mediation, and arbitration, with both parties presenting their proposals and bargaining for mutually acceptable terms."

A student named Marcus raised his hand. "What are some common issues negotiated in collective bargaining?"

"Common issues negotiated in collective bargaining include wages, benefits, hours of work, job security, and workplace safety," Dr. Hayes replied. "Both management and labor unions seek to reach agreements that balance the interests of employees with the operational needs of the organization."

He clicked to the next slide, which displayed the phrase: "Managing Labor Relations."

"Managing labor relations requires effective communication, collaboration, and conflict resolution skills," Dr. Hayes said. "Governments must foster positive relationships with labor unions, address employee concerns, and comply with labor laws and regulations to maintain productive working environments."

As the lecture continued, Dr. Hayes guided his students through examples of labor relations and collective bargaining in public administration, highlighting successful negotiation strategies and the impact of labor agreements on organizational performance.

"As you explore labor relations and collective bargaining," Dr. Hayes concluded, "consider the challenges and opportunities they present for governments in managing their workforce and fostering collaborative and productive relationships with employees."

The students left the lecture hall, intrigued by the intricacies of labor relations in the public sector. Dr. Hayes watched them go, feeling a sense of satisfaction at having shed light on this essential aspect of human resource management.

Diversity and Inclusion in the Public Sector

Dr. Robert Hayes entered the classroom with a sense of purpose, ready to explore the critical importance of diversity and inclusion in the public sector. This aspect of human resource management was vital for understanding how governments promote equality, foster inclusivity, and harness the benefits of a diverse workforce.

"Good morning, class," Dr. Hayes greeted, his voice infused with warmth. "Today, we delve into the realm of diversity and inclusion in the public sector, examining how governments embrace diversity, foster inclusion, and cultivate a culture of belonging among their employees."

He clicked to the first slide, revealing the title: "Diversity and Inclusion in the Public Sector."

"Diversity," Dr. Hayes began, "encompasses the variety of backgrounds, experiences, and perspectives that individuals bring to the workplace. Inclusion is the practice of ensuring that all employees feel valued, respected, and empowered to contribute their unique talents and insights."

As he spoke, images of diverse teams, inclusive workplaces, and employee resource groups filled the screen, illustrating the richness and vitality that diversity and inclusion bring to organizations.

"The first aspect of diversity and inclusion is diversity recruitment," Dr. Hayes continued. "Governments actively recruit and hire employees from diverse backgrounds to reflect the communities they serve and bring a range of perspectives to decision-making."

A hand shot up from a student named Emily. "How do governments promote diversity in recruitment?"

"Governments promote diversity in recruitment through targeted outreach efforts, diversity-focused job postings, and partnerships with community organizations," Dr. Hayes replied. "They also implement fair and unbiased selection processes to ensure equal opportunities for all candidates."

He clicked to the next slide, which read: "Inclusive Workplace Practices."

"The next aspect of diversity and inclusion is fostering an inclusive workplace culture," Dr. Hayes explained. "Governments create environments where all employees feel welcomed, respected, and valued for their contributions."

A student named Marcus raised his hand. "How do governments promote inclusion in the workplace?"

"Governments promote inclusion through policies and practices that support diversity, equity, and belonging," Dr. Hayes replied. "These may include diversity training, employee resource groups, mentorship programs, and flexible work arrangements that accommodate diverse needs and preferences."

He clicked to the next slide, which displayed the phrase: "Advancing Equity and Fairness."

"Advancing equity and fairness is essential for creating a workplace where all employees have equal opportunities to succeed," Dr. Hayes said. "Governments must address systemic barriers to diversity and inclusion, promote pay equity, and provide opportunities for professional growth and advancement for all employees."

As the lecture continued, Dr. Hayes guided his students through examples of diversity and inclusion initiatives in the public sector, highlighting their impact on employee engagement, organizational performance, and public service delivery.

"As you explore diversity and inclusion," Dr. Hayes concluded, "consider the role they play in fostering innovation, enhancing decision-making, and strengthening public trust in government institutions."

The students left the lecture hall, inspired by the possibilities of creating inclusive and diverse workplaces. Dr. Hayes watched them go, feeling a sense of optimism for the future of equity and fairness in the public sector.

Case Studies in Public HRM

Dr. Robert Hayes, with a stack of case studies in hand, entered the classroom, eager to delve into real-world examples of human resource management (HRM) in the public sector. This segment was essential for understanding how HRM principles were applied in practice to address challenges and seize opportunities in government organizations.

"Good morning, class," Dr. Hayes greeted, his voice filled with anticipation. "Today, we embark on a journey through case studies in public HRM, exploring how governments navigate complex HRM issues and implement innovative solutions to enhance workforce performance and organizational effectiveness."

He placed the case studies on the desk, each one representing a unique HRM challenge faced by a government agency.

"The first case study," Dr. Hayes began, "examines the implementation of a diversity recruitment initiative by a state government agency. Faced with a lack of diversity in its workforce, the agency developed targeted recruitment strategies to attract candidates from underrepresented backgrounds."

As he spoke, images of recruitment fairs, diversity outreach events, and inclusive job postings filled the screen, illustrating the agency's efforts to build a more diverse and inclusive workforce.

"The second case study," Dr. Hayes continued, "explores

the introduction of flexible work arrangements by a municipal government. Recognizing the need to accommodate employees' diverse needs and preferences, the government implemented telecommuting and flexible scheduling options."

A hand shot up from a student named Emily. "How did the flexible work arrangements impact employee satisfaction and productivity?"

"The flexible work arrangements led to increased employee satisfaction, improved work-life balance, and enhanced productivity," Dr. Hayes replied. "Employees reported greater job satisfaction and engagement, resulting in higher levels of performance and organizational commitment."

He clicked to the next slide, which read: "Lessons Learned."

"From these case studies, we can glean several lessons," Dr. Hayes explained. "The importance of proactive HRM strategies, tailored to the unique needs and challenges of government organizations. These case studies demonstrate the impact of HRM practices on employee morale, performance, and organizational effectiveness."

A student named Marcus raised his hand. "What other case studies will we explore?"

"We will explore a range of case studies covering various aspects of HRM, including performance management, employee development, and labor relations," Dr. Hayes replied. "Each case study offers valuable insights into the complexities of HRM in the public sector and the strategies governments employ to address HRM challenges and opportunities."

He clicked to the next slide, which displayed the phrase: "Applying Lessons to Practice."

"As you analyze these case studies," Dr. Hayes said, "consider how the lessons learned can be applied to real-world HRM situations, informing your understanding of effective HRM practices and guiding your future roles as public administrators."

As the lecture continued, Dr. Hayes guided his students through a series of case studies, encouraging them to critically analyze each example and draw connections to the principles and practices of HRM discussed in class.

"As you study these case studies," Dr. Hayes concluded, "consider the role HRM plays in shaping organizational culture, driving employee engagement, and advancing the mission of government agencies."

The students left the lecture hall, inspired by the practical applications of HRM in the public sector. Dr. Hayes watched them go, feeling a sense of satisfaction at having illuminated the complexities of HRM through real-world examples.

7

Chapter 7: Ethics and Accountability in Public Administration

Ethical Theories and Principles

Dr. Robert Hayes entered the classroom, his demeanor serious yet inviting, ready to explore the foundational principles of ethics and accountability in public administration. This segment was crucial for understanding the moral obligations and responsibilities of government officials in serving the public interest.

"Good morning, class," Dr. Hayes greeted, his voice carrying the weight of importance. "Today, we embark on a journey into the realm of ethics and accountability in public administration, examining the ethical theories and principles that guide decision-making and behavior in government."

He clicked to the first slide, unveiling the title: "Ethical Theories and Principles."

"Ethical theories," Dr. Hayes began, "provide frameworks for analyzing moral dilemmas and guiding ethical decision-making. Principles, on the other hand, are fundamental beliefs that govern conduct and define what is right and wrong."

As he spoke, images of philosophers, ethical dilemmas, and government officials in contemplation filled the screen, setting the stage for a deep dive into the complexities of ethical reasoning.

"The first aspect of ethics is understanding ethical theories," Dr. Hayes continued. "Ethical theories such as utilitarianism, deontology, and virtue ethics offer different perspectives on how to determine what is morally right or wrong."

A hand shot up from a student named Emily. "How do these theories apply to decision-making in public administration?"

"Ethical theories provide frameworks for evaluating the consequences of actions, the moral duties involved, and the character traits of individuals," Dr. Hayes replied. "In public administration, officials must consider the broader implications of their decisions on society, uphold ethical principles, and act with integrity and transparency."

He clicked to the next slide, which read: "Core Ethical Principles."

"The next aspect of ethics is understanding core ethical principles," Dr. Hayes explained. "These principles, such as honesty, fairness, integrity, and respect for others, serve as guiding values in public administration and shape the behavior of government officials."

A student named Marcus raised his hand. "How do governments promote ethical behavior among public servants?"

"Governments promote ethical behavior through codes of conduct, ethics training, and oversight mechanisms," Dr. Hayes replied. "They establish clear expectations for ethical conduct, provide guidance on navigating ethical dilemmas, and hold individuals accountable for their actions."

He clicked to the next slide, which displayed the phrase: "Upholding Public Trust."

"Upholding public trust is paramount in public administration," Dr. Hayes said. "Government officials must act ethically to maintain the confidence and trust of the public they serve, ensuring transparency, accountability, and integrity in all aspects of governance."

As the lecture continued, Dr. Hayes guided his students through examples of ethical theories and principles in public administration, illustrating their application in real-world scenarios and decision-making processes.

"As you explore ethical theories and principles," Dr. Hayes concluded, "consider the role they play in shaping the ethical culture of government organizations and the responsibilities they entail for public servants in upholding the highest standards of integrity and accountability."

The students left the lecture hall, contemplating the profound implications of ethics in public administration. Dr. Hayes watched them go, feeling a sense of satisfaction at having ignited their awareness of the ethical dimensions of governance.

Code of Conduct for Public Servants

Dr. Robert Hayes, with a sense of gravity, entered the classroom, prepared to delve into the importance of codes of conduct for public servants. This segment was crucial for understanding the standards of behavior expected from government officials and the mechanisms in place to ensure ethical conduct.

"Good morning, class," Dr. Hayes greeted, his voice resonating with solemnity. "Today, we continue our exploration of ethics and accountability in public administration by examining the significance of codes of conduct for public servants."

He clicked to the first slide, revealing the title: "Code of Conduct for Public Servants."

"A code of conduct," Dr. Hayes began, "is a set of ethical guidelines and standards that outline the expectations for behavior and conduct of public servants in fulfilling their duties."

As he spoke, images of government officials taking oaths, signing documents, and upholding values of integrity filled the screen, illustrating the solemn commitment to ethical conduct.

"The first aspect of a code of conduct is establishing ethical principles," Dr. Hayes continued. "These principles, such as honesty, impartiality, accountability, and respect for the law, serve as the foundation for ethical behavior in public service."

A hand shot up from a student named Emily. "How are codes of conduct developed and enforced?"

"Codes of conduct are typically developed through a collaborative process involving government agencies, ethics commissions, and stakeholders," Dr. Hayes replied. "They are enforced through oversight mechanisms, such as ethics boards, disciplinary procedures, and legal sanctions, to ensure compliance and accountability."

He clicked to the next slide, which read: "Adherence to Ethical Standards."

"The next aspect of a code of conduct is adherence to ethical standards," Dr. Hayes explained. "Public servants are expected to uphold the principles outlined in the code in all aspects of their work, including decision-making, interactions with stakeholders, and use of public resources."

A student named Marcus raised his hand. "How do codes of conduct promote ethical behavior in government?"

"Codes of conduct promote ethical behavior by setting clear expectations, providing guidance on ethical dilemmas, and establishing consequences for misconduct," Dr. Hayes replied. "They serve as a reminder of the responsibilities and obligations of public servants to act in the public interest and uphold the trust placed in them by society."

He clicked to the next slide, which displayed the phrase: "Building Public Trust."

"Building public trust is essential for effective governance," Dr. Hayes said. "Codes of conduct play a vital role in building and maintaining public trust by demonstrating the commitment of government officials to ethical conduct, integrity, and accountability."

As the lecture continued, Dr. Hayes guided his students through examples of codes of conduct in public administration, highlighting their role in promoting ethical behavior and maintaining public confidence in government institutions.

"As you explore codes of conduct," Dr. Hayes concluded, "consider the significance of ethical standards in ensuring the integrity and credibility of public service, and the responsibilities they entail for public servants in upholding the highest standards of ethical conduct."

The students left the lecture hall, reflecting on the profound impact of codes of conduct on ethical governance. Dr. Hayes watched them go, feeling a sense of assurance that they had grasped the importance of ethical standards in public administration.

Mechanisms for Accountability and Transparency

Dr. Robert Hayes entered the classroom, his expression earnest, ready to delve into the mechanisms for accountability and transparency in public administration. This segment was pivotal for understanding how governments ensure integrity, openness, and trustworthiness in their operations.

"Good morning, class," Dr. Hayes greeted, his voice carrying a tone of resolve. "Today, we continue our exploration of ethics and accountability in public administration by examining the mechanisms that uphold transparency and accountability in government."

He clicked to the first slide, unveiling the title: "Mechanisms for Accountability and Transparency."

"Mechanisms for accountability and transparency," Dr. Hayes began, "are essential for ensuring that government actions are conducted ethically, openly, and in the public interest."

As he spoke, images of oversight bodies, public hearings, and open data initiatives filled the screen, illustrating the diverse array of mechanisms used to foster accountability and transparency.

"The first aspect of accountability and transparency is oversight bodies," Dr. Hayes continued. "These bodies, such as ethics commissions, audit committees, and ombudsman offices, provide independent review and oversight of government operations."

A hand shot up from a student named Emily. "How do oversight bodies hold government officials accountable?"

"Oversight bodies hold government officials accountable by investigating complaints of misconduct, conducting audits and investigations, and recommending corrective actions or sanctions," Dr. Hayes replied. "They serve as watchdogs, ensuring that government actions are lawful, ethical, and in the public interest."

He clicked to the next slide, which read: "Public Access to Information."

"The next aspect of accountability and transparency is public access to information," Dr. Hayes explained. "Governments provide access to information through freedom of information laws, open data initiatives, and public disclosure requirements, enabling citizens to hold government officials accountable and participate in the democratic process."

A student named Marcus raised his hand. "How does public access to information promote transparency?"

"Public access to information promotes transparency by allowing citizens to scrutinize government actions, monitor decision-making processes, and hold officials accountable for their actions," Dr. Hayes replied. "It enhances public trust in government institutions and fosters a culture of openness and accountability."

He clicked to the next slide, which displayed the phrase: "Ethics Training and Education."

"The final aspect of accountability and transparency is ethics training and education," Dr. Hayes said. "Governments provide training and education programs to raise awareness of ethical standards, promote ethical decision-making, and empower public servants to act with integrity and professionalism."

As the lecture continued, Dr. Hayes guided his students

through examples of mechanisms for accountability and transparency in public administration, highlighting their role in promoting ethical conduct and maintaining public trust.

"As you explore mechanisms for accountability and transparency," Dr. Hayes concluded, "consider the importance of these mechanisms in upholding the principles of ethics and ensuring the integrity and credibility of government institutions."

The students left the lecture hall, pondering the profound implications of accountability and transparency in governance. Dr. Hayes watched them go, feeling a sense of assurance that they had grasped the importance of these principles in promoting ethical governance.

Corruption and Anti-Corruption Strategies

Dr. Robert Hayes entered the classroom, his expression grave, prepared to delve into the critical topic of corruption and anti-corruption strategies in public administration. This segment was vital for understanding the pervasive threat corruption poses to government integrity and the measures taken to combat it.

"Good morning, class," Dr. Hayes greeted, his voice tinged with seriousness. "Today, we confront the scourge of corruption and explore the strategies employed to combat it in public administration."

He clicked to the first slide, unveiling the title: "Corruption and Anti-Corruption Strategies."

"Corruption," Dr. Hayes began, "is the abuse of entrusted power for private gain, eroding public trust, distorting decision-making, and undermining the effectiveness of government institutions."

As he spoke, images of bribery, embezzlement, and kickbacks filled the screen, illustrating the various forms corruption can take and its detrimental impact on society.

"The first aspect we must address is understanding the root causes of corruption," Dr. Hayes continued. "Factors such as weak institutional governance, lack of transparency, impunity, and inadequate oversight create fertile ground for corrupt practices to thrive."

A hand shot up from a student named Emily. "How do governments combat corruption?"

"Governments combat corruption through a multifaceted approach that includes prevention, detection, enforcement, and education," Dr. Hayes replied. "They implement anti-corruption strategies and measures to strengthen governance, enhance transparency, and hold corrupt individuals accountable for their actions."

He clicked to the next slide, which read: "Preventive Measures."

"The next aspect is preventive measures," Dr. Hayes explained. "Governments implement preventive measures such as ethics training, conflict of interest policies, financial disclosure requirements, and procurement reforms to mitigate the risk of corruption and promote ethical conduct."

A student named Marcus raised his hand. "How effective are these preventive measures in deterring corruption?"

"While preventive measures are essential, their effectiveness depends on robust enforcement, oversight, and a culture of accountability," Dr. Hayes replied. "Governments must continuously evaluate and strengthen their anti-corruption measures to adapt to evolving threats and challenges."

He clicked to the next slide, which displayed the phrase: "Enforcement and Prosecution."

"The final aspect is enforcement and prosecution," Dr. Hayes said. "Governments must enforce anti-corruption laws, investigate allegations of corruption, and prosecute offenders to ensure accountability and deterrence."

As the lecture continued, Dr. Hayes guided his students through examples of corruption and anti-corruption strategies in public administration, highlighting successful interventions and ongoing challenges in combating corruption.

"As you explore corruption and anti-corruption strategies," Dr. Hayes concluded, "consider the role they play in upholding the principles of ethics and accountability, and the collective responsibility we have in safeguarding the integrity of government institutions."

The students left the lecture hall, sobered by the realities of corruption and inspired by the efforts to combat it. Dr. Hayes watched them go, feeling a sense of determination that they would carry forth the torch in the fight against corruption.

Public Trust and Integrity

Dr. Robert Hayes entered the classroom, his demeanor reflective, prepared to explore the critical importance of public trust and integrity in public administration. This segment was pivotal for understanding the foundation of government legitimacy and the imperative of maintaining the public's confidence in governmental institutions.

"Good morning, class," Dr. Hayes greeted, his voice carrying a tone of solemnity. "Today, we delve into the cornerstone of effective governance: public trust and integrity."

He clicked to the first slide, unveiling the title: "Public Trust and Integrity."

"Public trust," Dr. Hayes began, "is the bedrock upon which government legitimacy rests. It is the confidence and faith that citizens place in their government to act in the public interest and uphold ethical standards."

As he spoke, images of citizens engaging with government officials, participating in democratic processes, and demonstrating trust filled the screen, illustrating the symbiotic relationship between the government and the governed.

"The first aspect we must consider is understanding the factors that influence public trust," Dr. Hayes continued. "Factors such as transparency, accountability, responsiveness, and integrity shape citizens' perceptions of government legitimacy and trustworthiness."

A hand shot up from a student named Emily. "How do governments cultivate and maintain public trust?"

"Governments cultivate and maintain public trust through transparency, accountability, responsiveness, and ethical conduct," Dr. Hayes replied. "They must demonstrate a commitment to integrity, uphold the rule of law, and engage citizens in decision-making processes to build and sustain public trust."

He clicked to the next slide, which read: "Integrity in Action."

"The next aspect is integrity in action," Dr. Hayes explained. "Integrity is the adherence to ethical principles and values, even when faced with challenges or temptations. Governments must foster a culture of integrity, where ethical conduct is valued and rewarded."

A student named Marcus raised his hand. "How does

integrity contribute to effective governance?"

"Integrity contributes to effective governance by promoting trust, accountability, and legitimacy," Dr. Hayes replied. "When government officials act with integrity, citizens have confidence that their interests are being served, leading to greater cooperation, compliance, and public satisfaction with government institutions."

He clicked to the next slide, which displayed the phrase: "Erosion of Trust."

"The erosion of public trust," Dr. Hayes said somberly, "can have dire consequences for government legitimacy and democracy. Scandals, corruption, and breaches of trust can undermine citizens' confidence in their government and weaken the social contract between the governed and the governing."

As the lecture continued, Dr. Hayes guided his students through examples of public trust and integrity in public administration, highlighting the challenges and opportunities in fostering a culture of trustworthiness and ethical conduct.

"As you explore public trust and integrity," Dr. Hayes concluded, "consider the profound impact they have on government legitimacy, citizen engagement, and the health of democracy. Upholding these principles is not just a duty but a sacred responsibility of government officials."

The students left the lecture hall, contemplating the profound implications of public trust and integrity in governance. Dr. Hayes watched them go, feeling a sense of urgency that they would carry forth the torch in upholding these principles in their future roles as public servants.

Case Studies in Public Ethics

Dr. Robert Hayes entered the classroom, his demeanor poised, ready to delve into the practical applications of ethics in public administration through case studies. This segment was instrumental for understanding how ethical principles were upheld—or compromised—in real-world scenarios, guiding the moral compass of future public servants.

"Good morning, class," Dr. Hayes greeted, his voice infused with anticipation. "Today, we illuminate the complexities of public ethics through compelling case studies, exploring the ethical dilemmas faced by government officials and the decisions they make in navigating these challenges."

He clicked to the first slide, unveiling the title: "Case Studies in Public Ethics."

"Case studies," Dr. Hayes began, "provide invaluable insights into the application of ethical principles in the context of public administration. They allow us to examine ethical dilemmas, consider alternative courses of action, and reflect on the consequences of decisions made."

As he spoke, images of government officials, citizens, and stakeholders engaged in ethical deliberations filled the screen, setting the stage for a deep dive into the ethical complexities of governance.

"The first case study we'll explore," Dr. Hayes continued, "involves a procurement decision faced by a government agency. The agency must choose between awarding a contract to a vendor with political connections or selecting a vendor with a superior bid but no political ties."

A hand shot up from a student named Emily. "How do ethical considerations influence this decision?"

"Ethical considerations play a crucial role in this decision," Dr. Hayes replied. "Government officials must prioritize the public interest over personal or political interests, ensuring fairness, transparency, and integrity in the procurement process."

He clicked to the next slide, which read: "Ethical Decision-Making Framework."

"The next case study," Dr. Hayes explained, "centers on a conflict of interest situation faced by a public official. The official must recuse themselves from a decision-making process involving a company in which they have a financial interest."

A student named Marcus raised his hand. "What ethical principles guide the official's decision?"

"The official must adhere to ethical principles such as integrity, accountability, and transparency," Dr. Hayes replied. "They must act in the best interests of the public and avoid any actions that could undermine trust or compromise their impartiality."

He clicked to the next slide, which displayed the phrase: "Lessons Learned."

"As we analyze these case studies," Dr. Hayes said, "we must consider the lessons learned and the implications for ethical conduct in public administration. These case studies offer valuable insights into the complexities of ethical decision-making and the challenges of upholding integrity and trust in government."

As the lecture continued, Dr. Hayes guided his students through a series of case studies, encouraging them to critically analyze each scenario and apply ethical principles to proposed solutions.

"As you explore these case studies," Dr. Hayes concluded, "consider the responsibilities of government officials in upholding ethical standards and the importance of ethical leadership in fostering trust and confidence in government institutions."

The students left the lecture hall, enriched by the practical applications of ethics in public administration. Dr. Hayes watched them go, feeling a sense of pride in their growing understanding of the complexities of ethical governance.

$$8$$

Chapter 8: Public Sector Leadership

Leadership Theories and Styles

D r. Robert Hayes strode into the classroom with purpose, ready to embark on a journey into the dynamic realm of public sector leadership. This segment was pivotal for understanding the theories and styles that underpin effective leadership in government, shaping the course of public policy and administration.

"Good morning, class," Dr. Hayes greeted, his voice resonating with enthusiasm. "Today, we delve into the heart of leadership in the public sector, exploring the theories and styles that guide the actions of government officials in shaping the future of governance."

He clicked to the first slide, unveiling the title: "Leadership Theories and Styles."

"Leadership," Dr. Hayes began, "is the art of influencing and inspiring others to achieve common goals. In the public sector, effective leadership is essential for driving innovation, fostering collaboration, and delivering results for the public good."

As he spoke, images of iconic leaders, from presidents to civil servants, flashed on the screen, representing the diverse array of leadership styles and approaches.

"The first aspect we must consider is understanding leadership theories," Dr. Hayes continued. "Leadership theories provide frameworks for understanding the nature of leadership, the traits and behaviors of effective leaders, and the dynamics of leadership in different contexts."

A hand shot up from a student named Emily. "What are some examples of leadership theories?"

"Leadership theories range from trait theories, which focus on the inherent characteristics of leaders, to contingency theories, which emphasize the situational factors that influence leadership effectiveness," Dr. Hayes replied. "Other theories include transformational leadership, servant leadership, and authentic leadership, each offering unique insights into the dynamics of leadership in the public sector."

He clicked to the next slide, which read: "Leadership Styles."

"The next aspect is leadership styles," Dr. Hayes explained. "Leadership styles reflect the approach and behaviors that leaders adopt in guiding and directing their teams. Common leadership styles include autocratic, democratic, laissez-faire, and transactional leadership."

A student named Marcus raised his hand. "How do leadership styles impact government effectiveness?"

"Leadership styles can have a significant impact on government effectiveness," Dr. Hayes replied. "Democratic leadership, for example, promotes participation and collaboration, fostering innovation and buy-in from stakeholders.

In contrast, autocratic leadership may lead to resentment and resistance, hindering progress and eroding trust."

He clicked to the next slide, which displayed the phrase: "Adaptive Leadership."

"The final aspect we'll explore is adaptive leadership," Dr. Hayes said. "Adaptive leaders excel in navigating complex and uncertain environments, embracing change, and empowering others to adapt and thrive in challenging circumstances."

As the lecture continued, Dr. Hayes guided his students through examples of leadership theories and styles in the public sector, illustrating their application in government decision-making and organizational dynamics.

"As you explore leadership theories and styles," Dr. Hayes concluded, "consider the importance of adaptive leadership in addressing the evolving challenges of governance and the role of effective leadership in driving positive change for the public good."

The students left the lecture hall, inspired by the myriad possibilities of leadership in the public sector. Dr. Hayes watched them go, feeling a sense of optimism for the future of governance under their capable hands.

Decision Making and Problem Solving

Dr. Robert Hayes entered the classroom, his presence commanding attention as he prepared to delve into the intricacies of decision making and problem solving in public sector leadership. This segment was pivotal for understanding how leaders navigate complex challenges and make critical decisions to shape the course of governance.

"Good morning, class," Dr. Hayes greeted, his voice resonating with authority. "Today, we explore the essence of leadership in decision making and problem solving, uncovering the strategies and approaches that guide leaders in addressing the myriad challenges of governance."

He clicked to the first slide, unveiling the title: "Decision Making and Problem Solving."

"Decision making," Dr. Hayes began, "is the process of selecting a course of action from among multiple alternatives. In the public sector, leaders must make decisions that balance competing interests, address complex issues, and uphold the public good."

As he spoke, images of leaders analyzing data, engaging in deliberation, and weighing options filled the screen, illustrating the dynamic nature of decision making in government.

"The first aspect we must consider is understanding the decision-making process," Dr. Hayes continued. "The decision-making process typically involves identifying a problem, gathering information, analyzing alternatives, making a choice, and implementing and evaluating the decision."

A hand shot up from a student named Emily. "How do leaders ensure effective decision making in government?"

"Effective decision making in government requires leaders to employ systematic approaches, engage stakeholders, and consider the long-term implications of their decisions," Dr. Hayes replied. "They must foster a culture of transparency, accountability, and collaboration to ensure that decisions are informed, equitable, and aligned with the public interest."

He clicked to the next slide, which read: "Problem Solving Strategies."

"The next aspect is problem solving strategies," Dr. Hayes

explained. "Problem solving involves identifying, analyzing, and resolving challenges to achieve desired outcomes. Leaders employ various strategies, such as root cause analysis, brainstorming, and consensus building, to address complex issues and drive solutions."

A student named Marcus raised his hand. "How do leaders overcome obstacles in problem solving?"

"Leaders overcome obstacles in problem solving by fostering creativity, resilience, and innovation," Dr. Hayes replied. "They encourage diverse perspectives, embrace experimentation, and leverage technology and data to develop effective solutions to complex problems."

He clicked to the next slide, which displayed the phrase: "Ethical Considerations."

"The final aspect we'll explore is ethical considerations in decision making and problem solving," Dr. Hayes said. "Leaders must consider the ethical implications of their decisions, ensuring fairness, integrity, and accountability in their actions."

As the lecture continued, Dr. Hayes guided his students through examples of decision making and problem solving in the public sector, highlighting the importance of ethical leadership and strategic thinking in addressing governance challenges.

"As you explore decision making and problem solving," Dr. Hayes concluded, "consider the role of effective leadership in driving positive change and advancing the public interest. Leadership in government requires vision, courage, and a commitment to excellence in serving the needs of the people."

The students left the lecture hall, inspired by the possibilities of leadership in addressing societal challenges. Dr. Hayes watched them go, feeling a sense of pride in their growing understanding of the complexities of governance and the role of leadership in shaping the future.

Crisis Management and Resilience

Dr. Robert Hayes entered the classroom, his demeanor composed yet resolute, prepared to delve into the critical topic of crisis management and resilience in public sector leadership. This segment was essential for understanding how leaders navigate turbulent times, inspire confidence, and steer their organizations through adversity.

"Good morning, class," Dr. Hayes greeted, his voice projecting calm authority. "Today, we confront the challenges of crisis management and resilience in public sector leadership, exploring the strategies and principles that guide leaders in times of uncertainty and upheaval."

He clicked to the first slide, unveiling the title: "Crisis Management and Resilience."

"Crisis management," Dr. Hayes began, "is the process of identifying, mitigating, and resolving crises to minimize their impact on organizational objectives and stakeholders. Resilience, on the other hand, is the ability to adapt and recover from adversity, emerging stronger and more capable than before."

As he spoke, images of leaders coordinating disaster response efforts, communicating with the public, and demonstrating resolve filled the screen, illustrating the multifaceted nature of crisis management and resilience in government.

"The first aspect we must consider is understanding the nature of crises," Dr. Hayes continued. "Crises can take many forms, including natural disasters, public health emergencies, economic downturns, and social unrest. Effective crisis management requires leaders to anticipate potential crises, develop response plans, and mobilize resources to address them swiftly and effectively."

A hand shot up from a student named Emily. "How do leaders maintain resilience in the face of crises?"

"Leaders maintain resilience by fostering a culture of preparedness, adaptability, and collaboration," Dr. Hayes replied. "They must inspire confidence, provide clear direction, and communicate transparently with stakeholders to navigate crises and instill hope for the future."

He clicked to the next slide, which read: "Crisis Response Strategies."

"The next aspect is crisis response strategies," Dr. Hayes explained. "Leaders employ various strategies, such as risk assessment, emergency response planning, crisis communication, and resource mobilization, to manage crises effectively and protect the interests of their organizations and communities."

A student named Marcus raised his hand. "How do leaders ensure effective communication during crises?"

"Effective communication during crises requires leaders to be transparent, timely, and empathetic," Dr. Hayes replied. "They must provide accurate information, address public concerns, and demonstrate empathy for those affected by the crisis. Communication fosters trust, enhances coordination, and enables stakeholders to make informed decisions in challenging circumstances."

He clicked to the next slide, which displayed the phrase: "Building Back Better."

"The final aspect we'll explore is the concept of 'building back better,'" Dr. Hayes said. "Crisis management is not just about responding to immediate challenges but also about seizing opportunities for innovation, growth, and renewal. Leaders must leverage lessons learned from crises to strengthen their organizations, enhance resilience, and build a more sustainable future."

As the lecture continued, Dr. Hayes guided his students through examples of crisis management and resilience in the public sector, highlighting successful strategies and lessons learned from past crises.

"As you explore crisis management and resilience," Dr. Hayes concluded, "consider the role of effective leadership in guiding organizations through adversity and inspiring confidence in the face of uncertainty. Leadership in crisis requires courage, compassion, and a commitment to serving the public interest."

The students left the lecture hall, contemplating the profound challenges and opportunities of crisis management and resilience. Dr. Hayes watched them go, feeling a sense of determination that they would carry forth the lessons learned into their future roles as public sector leaders.

Communication and Public Relations

Dr. Robert Hayes stepped into the classroom, his demeanor poised and ready to explore the vital realm of communication and public relations in public sector leadership. This segment was crucial for understanding how effective communication shapes perceptions, fosters trust, and enhances collaboration in government.

"Good morning, class," Dr. Hayes greeted, his voice carrying a tone of purpose. "Today, we dive into the essential components of communication and public relations in public sector leadership, unraveling the strategies and techniques that leaders employ to engage stakeholders and convey their vision."

He clicked to the first slide, unveiling the title: "Communication and Public Relations."

"Communication," Dr. Hayes began, "is the lifeblood of effective leadership. In the public sector, leaders must communicate transparently, clearly, and empathetically to inform, engage, and inspire action among stakeholders."

As he spoke, images of leaders addressing the public, interacting with constituents, and collaborating with colleagues filled the screen, illustrating the diverse dimensions of communication in government.

"The first aspect we must consider is understanding the importance of effective communication," Dr. Hayes continued. "Effective communication builds trust, fosters transparency, and enhances collaboration. It is the cornerstone of effective governance, enabling leaders to convey their priorities, address concerns, and mobilize support for initiatives."

A hand shot up from a student named Emily. "How do leaders ensure effective communication in government?"

"Leaders ensure effective communication by adopting a strategic approach, tailoring messages to diverse audiences, and utilizing multiple channels of communication," Dr. Hayes replied. "They must listen actively, engage stakeholders in dialogue, and communicate with empathy and authenticity to build rapport and credibility."

He clicked to the next slide, which read: "Public Relations

Strategies."

"The next aspect is public relations strategies," Dr. Hayes explained. "Public relations encompasses the strategies and tactics that organizations use to manage their reputation, build positive relationships with stakeholders, and communicate their mission and values effectively."

A student named Marcus raised his hand. "How do leaders manage public perception in government?"

"Leaders manage public perception by proactively engaging with the media, responding to inquiries and feedback, and leveraging opportunities to showcase their achievements and initiatives," Dr. Hayes replied. "They must be transparent, responsive, and accountable in their communications, earning the trust and confidence of the public."

He clicked to the next slide, which displayed the phrase: "Crisis Communication."

"The final aspect we'll explore is crisis communication," Dr. Hayes said. "Crisis communication involves communicating effectively during emergencies, addressing public concerns, and managing reputational risks. Leaders must be prepared to communicate swiftly, accurately, and compassionately to mitigate the impact of crises on stakeholders."

As the lecture continued, Dr. Hayes guided his students through examples of communication and public relations strategies in the public sector, highlighting successful approaches and best practices for engaging stakeholders and managing reputational risks.

"As you explore communication and public relations," Dr. Hayes concluded, "consider the profound impact they have on public trust, stakeholder engagement, and the effectiveness of government. Effective communication is not just a skill but a fundamental responsibility of leadership in the public sector."

The students left the lecture hall, inspired by the power of communication to shape perceptions and drive positive change. Dr. Hayes watched them go, feeling a sense of optimism for the future of governance under their capable hands.

Case Studies in Public Sector Leadership

Dr. Robert Hayes stood before the class, his demeanor reflective, ready to delve into the real-world applications of public sector leadership through compelling case studies. This segment was instrumental for understanding how leaders navigate complex challenges, make tough decisions, and inspire change in government.

"Good morning, class," Dr. Hayes greeted, his voice carrying a tone of anticipation. "Today, we embark on a journey through case studies in public sector leadership, exploring the triumphs, challenges, and lessons learned from leaders who have left their mark on governance."

He clicked to the first slide, unveiling the title: "Case Studies in Public Sector Leadership."

"Case studies," Dr. Hayes began, "offer invaluable insights into the complexities of leadership in government. They allow us to examine the strategies, decisions, and outcomes of leaders faced with real-world challenges, providing valuable lessons for aspiring public servants."

As he spoke, images of iconic leaders, from presidents to local officials, flashed on the screen, representing the diverse array of leadership styles and approaches in government.

"The first case study we'll explore," Dr. Hayes continued,

"centers on the leadership of Mayor Maria Rodriguez during a major urban revitalization project. Mayor Rodriguez faced daunting challenges, from budget constraints to community opposition, as she sought to revitalize the city's downtown district."

A hand shot up from a student named Emily. "How did Mayor Rodriguez navigate these challenges?"

"Mayor Rodriguez navigated these challenges by engaging stakeholders, fostering collaboration, and demonstrating visionary leadership," Dr. Hayes replied. "She solicited input from residents, business owners, and community leaders, forging consensus around the revitalization plan and garnering support for her initiatives."

He clicked to the next slide, which read: "Leadership Lessons Learned."

"The next case study," Dr. Hayes explained, "involves the leadership of Dr. David Patel during a public health crisis. Dr. Patel faced the daunting task of managing a disease outbreak while balancing public health concerns, economic impacts, and political pressures."

A student named Marcus raised his hand. "How did Dr. Patel address these competing interests?"

"Dr. Patel addressed these competing interests by prioritizing public health, communicating transparently, and collaborating with stakeholders," Dr. Hayes replied. "He implemented evidence-based interventions, engaged with the media to provide accurate information, and worked closely with government agencies, healthcare providers, and community organizations to coordinate response efforts."

He clicked to the next slide, which displayed the phrase: "Leadership Impact."

"The final case study we'll explore," Dr. Hayes said, "centers on the leadership of Secretary Sarah Thompson in advancing environmental sustainability initiatives. Secretary Thompson faced resistance from industry stakeholders, political opposition, and budget constraints as she sought to implement ambitious environmental policies."

As the lecture continued, Dr. Hayes guided his students through examples of public sector leadership, highlighting successful strategies, leadership qualities, and the impact of leadership on governance outcomes.

"As you explore these case studies," Dr. Hayes concluded, "consider the leadership qualities, strategies, and decisions that contributed to success or failure in each scenario. Case studies offer valuable insights into the complexities of leadership in government and the enduring impact of effective leadership on society."

The students left the lecture hall, inspired by the leadership journeys of those who have shaped the course of governance. Dr. Hayes watched them go, feeling a sense of hope that they would carry forth the lessons learned into their future roles as public sector leaders.

9

Chapter 9: E-Government and Digital Administration

Introduction to E-Government

Dr. Robert Hayes entered the classroom, his enthusiasm palpable as he prepared to explore the transformative world of e-government and digital administration. This segment was pivotal for understanding how technology revolutionizes governance, enhances service delivery, and empowers citizens in the digital age.

"Good morning, class," Dr. Hayes greeted, his voice infused with excitement. "Today, we embark on a journey into the realm of e-government and digital administration, unraveling the opportunities and challenges of leveraging technology to enhance governance."

He clicked to the first slide, unveiling the title: "Introduction to E-Government."

"E-Government," Dr. Hayes began, "is the use of information and communication technologies (ICTs) to deliver government services, engage citizens, and improve the efficiency and effectiveness of government operations."

As he spoke, images of digital platforms, online services, and smart cities filled the screen, showcasing the myriad ways technology transforms the delivery of public services.

"The first aspect we must consider is understanding the evolution of e-government," Dr. Hayes continued. "E-Government has evolved from basic online services, such as websites and email communication, to more advanced applications, including e-procurement, digital identity systems, and data analytics."

A hand shot up from a student named Emily. "How does e-government benefit citizens?"

"E-Government benefits citizens by providing convenient access to services, enhancing transparency and accountability, and promoting civic engagement," Dr. Hayes replied. "Citizens can access government services anytime, anywhere, using digital channels, and participate in decision-making processes through online platforms and social media."

He clicked to the next slide, which read: "Key Components of E-Government."

"The next aspect is understanding the key components of e-government," Dr. Hayes explained. "E-Government encompasses a wide range of applications, including electronic service delivery, digital infrastructure, cybersecurity measures, and data management systems."

A student named Marcus raised his hand. "What are some examples of e-government initiatives?"

"Examples of e-government initiatives include online tax filing systems, electronic voting platforms, digital health records, and smart city technologies," Dr. Hayes replied. "These initiatives streamline government processes, improve service quality, and empower citizens to interact with government more efficiently."

He clicked to the next slide, which displayed the phrase: "Future Trends in E-Government."

"The final aspect we'll explore is the future trends in e-government," Dr. Hayes said. "As technology continues to evolve, e-government is poised to embrace innovations such as artificial intelligence, blockchain technology, and the Internet of Things, transforming governance in profound ways."

As the lecture continued, Dr. Hayes guided his students through examples of e-government initiatives around the world, highlighting successful strategies, challenges, and emerging trends in digital administration.

"As you explore e-government," Dr. Hayes concluded, "consider the potential of technology to empower governments, citizens, and communities in shaping a more inclusive, responsive, and effective governance. E-government is not just about technology; it's about leveraging technology to improve people's lives."

The students left the lecture hall, inspired by the possibilities of e-government to revolutionize governance. Dr. Hayes watched them go, feeling a sense of excitement for the digital future of governance under their capable hands.

Digital Transformation in Public Service

Dr. Robert Hayes stood at the front of the classroom, his demeanor charged with anticipation as he delved into the transformative power of digital technology in reshaping public service delivery. This segment was crucial for understanding how digital transformation revolutionizes the way governments interact with citizens and deliver services.

"Good morning, class," Dr. Hayes greeted, his voice brimming with enthusiasm. "Today, we explore the concept of digital transformation in public service, uncovering the innovative strategies and technologies that drive efficiency, accessibility, and responsiveness in government."

He clicked to the first slide, unveiling the title: "Digital Transformation in Public Service."

"Digital transformation," Dr. Hayes began, "is the integration of digital technologies into all aspects of government operations, from service delivery to policy making, to enhance efficiency, improve service quality, and meet the evolving needs of citizens."

As he spoke, images of government websites, mobile applications, and online portals filled the screen, illustrating the diverse array of digital tools and platforms used to engage citizens and streamline government processes.

"The first aspect we must consider is understanding the impact of digital transformation on public service delivery," Dr. Hayes continued. "Digital transformation enables governments to deliver services more efficiently, effectively, and conveniently, reducing bureaucracy, eliminating paper-based processes, and enhancing the overall citizen experience."

A hand shot up from a student named Emily. "How does digital transformation benefit citizens?"

"Digital transformation benefits citizens by providing access to services anytime, anywhere, using digital channels," Dr. Hayes replied. "Citizens can apply for permits, pay taxes, access information, and interact with government agencies online, saving time and reducing the need for in-person visits."

He clicked to the next slide, which read: "Key Drivers of Digital Transformation."

"The next aspect is understanding the key drivers of digital transformation," Dr. Hayes explained. "Digital transformation is driven by factors such as advances in technology, changing citizen expectations, government mandates, and the need to improve operational efficiency and cost-effectiveness."

A student named Marcus raised his hand. "What are some examples of digital transformation initiatives?"

"Examples of digital transformation initiatives include the development of digital government platforms, the adoption of cloud computing and data analytics, and the implementation of online service portals and mobile applications," Dr. Hayes replied. "These initiatives enable governments to deliver services more effectively, respond to citizen needs in real-time, and harness data to inform decision making."

He clicked to the next slide, which displayed the phrase: "Challenges and Opportunities."

"The final aspect we'll explore is the challenges and opportunities of digital transformation in public service," Dr. Hayes said. "While digital transformation offers immense potential for improving government efficiency and citizen satisfaction, it also presents challenges such as digital inequality, cybersecurity risks, and resistance to change."

As the lecture continued, Dr. Hayes guided his students through examples of digital transformation initiatives in public service delivery, highlighting successful strategies, emerging technologies, and best practices for leveraging digital tools to enhance governance.

"As you explore digital transformation," Dr. Hayes

concluded, "consider the role of technology in reshaping government-citizen interactions and the opportunities it presents for driving innovation, efficiency, and inclusivity in public service delivery. Digital transformation is not just a trend; it's a fundamental shift in how governments serve and engage with citizens in the digital age."

The students left the lecture hall, inspired by the potential of digital transformation to revolutionize governance. Dr. Hayes watched them go, feeling a sense of optimism for the future of public service in the digital era.

Data Management and Cybersecurity

Dr. Robert Hayes stood before the class, his expression serious yet determined as he delved into the critical aspects of data management and cybersecurity in the realm of e-government and digital administration. This segment was essential for understanding how governments safeguard sensitive information and maintain trust in an increasingly digital world.

"Good morning, class," Dr. Hayes greeted, his voice commanding attention. "Today, we confront the pressing issues of data management and cybersecurity in the context of e-government, exploring the strategies and protocols that governments employ to protect citizen data and secure their digital infrastructure."

He clicked to the first slide, unveiling the title: "Data Management and Cybersecurity."

"Data management," Dr. Hayes began, "is the process of collecting, storing, and utilizing data to inform decision making and enhance service delivery. In the digital age, governments must manage vast amounts of data while ensuring its accuracy, integrity, and confidentiality."

As he spoke, images of servers, data centers, and encrypted files filled the screen, illustrating the complexity of data management in government operations.

"The first aspect we must consider is understanding the importance of data management in e-government," Dr. Hayes continued. "Data management enables governments to analyze trends, identify opportunities, and optimize service delivery, ultimately improving efficiency and effectiveness in governance."

A hand shot up from a student named Emily. "How do governments ensure the security of citizen data?"

"Governments ensure the security of citizen data through robust cybersecurity measures," Dr. Hayes replied. "Cybersecurity encompasses the practices, technologies, and policies designed to protect digital systems, networks, and data from unauthorized access, cyberattacks, and data breaches."

He clicked to the next slide, which read: "Key Components of Cybersecurity."

"The next aspect is understanding the key components of cybersecurity," Dr. Hayes explained. "Cybersecurity involves measures such as encryption, access controls, network monitoring, and incident response planning to safeguard government systems and data from cyber threats."

A student named Marcus raised his hand. "What are some common cyber threats governments face?"

"Common cyber threats governments face include malware attacks, phishing scams, ransomware, and insider threats," Dr. Hayes replied. "These threats can compromise sensitive information, disrupt government operations, and undermine public trust in government institutions."

He clicked to the next slide, which displayed the phrase: "Building Cyber Resilience."

"The final aspect we'll explore is the concept of building cyber resilience," Dr. Hayes said. "Cyber resilience involves the ability to detect, respond to, and recover from cyberattacks while maintaining essential functions and services. Governments must prioritize cyber resilience to mitigate the impact of cyber threats and ensure the continuity of government operations."

As the lecture continued, Dr. Hayes guided his students through examples of data management and cybersecurity practices in government, highlighting successful strategies, emerging technologies, and best practices for protecting citizen data and digital infrastructure.

"As you explore data management and cybersecurity," Dr. Hayes concluded, "consider the critical role they play in maintaining trust, integrity, and accountability in e-government. Data is a valuable asset, and safeguarding it is paramount to preserving public confidence in government institutions."

The students left the lecture hall, contemplating the profound implications of data management and cybersecurity in the digital age. Dr. Hayes watched them go, feeling a sense of urgency to equip them with the knowledge and skills needed to navigate the complexities of e-government in a rapidly evolving landscape.

Citizen Engagement through Digital Platforms

Dr. Robert Hayes paced the front of the classroom, his energy palpable as he delved into the dynamic realm of citizen engagement through digital platforms. This segment was pivotal for understanding how governments harness technology to foster transparency, participation, and collaboration with citizens in governance.

"Good morning, class," Dr. Hayes greeted, his voice brimming with enthusiasm. "Today, we explore the exciting landscape of citizen engagement through digital platforms, unraveling the transformative power of technology in connecting governments and citizens in meaningful ways."

He clicked to the first slide, unveiling the title: "Citizen Engagement through Digital Platforms."

"Citizen engagement," Dr. Hayes began, "is the process of involving citizens in government decision making, policy development, and service delivery. Digital platforms offer governments innovative tools to engage citizens, solicit feedback, and co-create solutions to complex challenges."

As he spoke, images of social media platforms, online forums, and interactive websites filled the screen, showcasing the diverse array of digital tools used to facilitate citizen participation in governance.

"The first aspect we must consider is understanding the importance of citizen engagement in e-government," Dr. Hayes continued. "Citizen engagement fosters transparency, accountability, and trust in government by giving citizens a voice in decision making and enabling them to contribute to the policy process."

A hand shot up from a student named Emily. "How do governments effectively engage citizens through digital platforms?"

"Governments effectively engage citizens through digital platforms by providing accessible, user-friendly channels for participation," Dr. Hayes replied. "This includes interactive websites, social media platforms, mobile applications, and online forums where citizens can provide feedback, participate in surveys, and collaborate with government officials and fellow citizens."

He clicked to the next slide, which read: "Key Strategies for Citizen Engagement."

"The next aspect is understanding the key strategies for citizen engagement through digital platforms," Dr. Hayes explained. "These strategies include targeted outreach campaigns, online consultations, virtual town hall meetings, crowdsourcing initiatives, and digital feedback mechanisms to ensure diverse and inclusive participation."

A student named Marcus raised his hand. "What are some examples of successful citizen engagement initiatives?"

"Examples of successful citizen engagement initiatives include participatory budgeting projects, online policy consultations, civic hackathons, and crowdsourced decision-making processes," Dr. Hayes replied. "These initiatives empower citizens to contribute their expertise, insights, and ideas to inform government policies and programs."

He clicked to the next slide, which displayed the phrase: "Measuring Impact."

"The final aspect we'll explore is measuring the impact of citizen engagement through digital platforms," Dr. Hayes said. "Governments must evaluate the effectiveness of their engagement efforts, measure citizen satisfaction and participation rates, and use data-driven insights to improve their digital engagement strategies over time."

As the lecture continued, Dr. Hayes guided his students through examples of citizen engagement initiatives facilitated by digital platforms, highlighting successful strategies, challenges, and best practices for promoting meaningful participation in governance.

"As you explore citizen engagement through digital platforms," Dr. Hayes concluded, "consider the transformative potential of technology to bridge the gap between governments and citizens, empower grassroots activism, and foster a culture of collaboration and inclusivity in governance. Digital engagement is not just about technology; it's about building stronger, more responsive democracies."

The students left the lecture hall, inspired by the possibilities of digital platforms to empower citizen participation in governance. Dr. Hayes watched them go, feeling a sense of optimism for the future of democracy in the digital age.

Challenges of Implementing E-Government

Dr. Robert Hayes stood before the class, his demeanor serious yet resolute as he delved into the formidable challenges of implementing e-government initiatives. This segment was crucial for understanding the complexities and obstacles governments face in harnessing technology to transform governance.

"Good morning, class," Dr. Hayes greeted, his voice carrying a tone of gravitas. "Today, we confront the daunting challenges of implementing e-government initiatives, unraveling the barriers and hurdles that governments must overcome to realize the full potential of digital transformation."

He clicked to the first slide, unveiling the title: "Challenges of Implementing E-Government."

"E-Government," Dr. Hayes began, "holds immense promise for improving government efficiency, enhancing service delivery, and empowering citizens. However, its implementation is not without its challenges."

As he spoke, images of bureaucratic red tape, technological barriers, and organizational resistance filled the screen, illustrating the multifaceted nature of the challenges governments encounter in adopting e-government initiatives.

"The first aspect we must consider is understanding the complexity of digital transformation," Dr. Hayes continued. "E-Government initiatives often require significant investments in technology infrastructure, workforce training, and organizational restructuring, posing logistical and financial challenges for governments."

A hand shot up from a student named Emily. "How do governments address the challenge of digital divide?"

"Governments address the challenge of the digital divide by ensuring equitable access to digital services and technologies," Dr. Hayes replied. "This includes bridging the gap in digital literacy, providing internet connectivity to underserved communities, and designing user-friendly interfaces to accommodate diverse user needs."

He clicked to the next slide, which read: "Organizational Resistance."

"The next aspect is organizational resistance to change," Dr. Hayes explained. "E-Government initiatives often encounter resistance from entrenched bureaucracies, legacy systems, and cultural barriers within government agencies, hindering the adoption and implementation of digital technologies."

A student named Marcus raised his hand. "How do governments overcome organizational resistance?"

"Governments overcome organizational resistance through leadership commitment, stakeholder engagement, and change management strategies," Dr. Hayes replied. "This includes fostering a culture of innovation, providing training and support for employees, and incentivizing adoption of e-government initiatives."

He clicked to the next slide, which displayed the phrase: "Cybersecurity Risks."

"The final aspect we'll explore is cybersecurity risks," Dr. Hayes said. "E-Government initiatives are vulnerable to cyber threats such as data breaches, ransomware attacks, and phishing scams, posing risks to citizen privacy, government operations, and public trust."

As the lecture continued, Dr. Hayes guided his students through examples of the challenges governments face in implementing e-government initiatives, highlighting strategies and best practices for overcoming these obstacles and ensuring the success of digital transformation efforts.

"As you explore the challenges of implementing e-government," Dr. Hayes concluded, "consider the importance of proactive planning, stakeholder engagement, and resilience in navigating the complexities of digital transformation. E-Government is not without its challenges, but with determination and strategic foresight, governments can harness technology to create a more efficient, inclusive, and responsive governance."

The students left the lecture hall, contemplative of the hurdles governments must overcome in embracing e-government initiatives. Dr. Hayes watched them go, feeling a sense of determination to equip them with the knowledge and skills needed to navigate the digital challenges of governance.

Case Studies in Digital Governance

Dr. Robert Hayes stood before the class, his voice filled with anticipation as he prepared to delve into real-world examples of digital governance in action. This segment was pivotal for understanding how governments around the world leverage technology to innovate and transform governance practices.

"Good morning, class," Dr. Hayes greeted, his tone infused with excitement. "Today, we explore case studies in digital governance, examining successful e-government initiatives from various countries and contexts."

He clicked to the first slide, unveiling the title: "Case Studies in Digital Governance."

"Digital governance," Dr. Hayes began, "encompasses a wide range of initiatives aimed at leveraging technology to improve government efficiency, enhance service delivery, and foster citizen engagement. Through case studies, we can gain insights into the strategies, challenges, and outcomes of digital governance initiatives."

As he spoke, images of innovative e-government projects from countries such as Estonia, Singapore, and South Korea filled the screen, showcasing the diversity of approaches and technologies used to drive digital transformation in governance.

"The first case study we'll explore is Estonia's e-Residency program," Dr. Hayes continued. "Estonia has pioneered digital governance with initiatives such as e-Residency, which allows individuals to establish and manage a business online from anywhere in the world. This program has attracted entrepreneurs, investors, and digital nomads, boosting Estonia's economy and global reputation as a leader in digital innovation."

A hand shot up from a student named Emily. "What are some key lessons from Estonia's e-Residency program?"

"Key lessons from Estonia's e-Residency program include the importance of digital infrastructure, trust in government institutions, and a supportive regulatory environment for innovation," Dr. Hayes replied. "By leveraging technology to simplify administrative processes and empower individuals, Estonia has demonstrated the transformative potential of e-government to drive economic growth and global competitiveness."

He clicked to the next slide, which read: "Singapore's Smart Nation Initiative."

"The next case study is Singapore's Smart Nation initiative," Dr. Hayes explained. "Singapore has embarked on a comprehensive effort to harness technology to improve urban living, enhance public services, and promote sustainability. Through initiatives such as digital identity, smart sensors, and data analytics, Singapore aims to create a seamless, efficient, and sustainable city for its citizens."

A student named Marcus raised his hand. "What are some challenges Singapore faces in implementing its Smart Nation initiative?"

"Challenges Singapore faces in implementing its Smart Nation initiative include data privacy concerns, cybersecurity risks, and ensuring equitable access to digital services," Dr. Hayes replied. "As Singapore embraces technology to transform governance, it must address these challenges to build trust, safeguard privacy, and ensure the benefits of digital innovation are accessible to all citizens."

He clicked to the next slide, which displayed the phrase:

"Lessons Learned."

"The final aspect we'll explore is lessons learned from these case studies," Dr. Hayes said. "By studying successful e-government initiatives, we can identify best practices, innovative strategies, and potential pitfalls to inform our own efforts in digital governance."

As the lecture continued, Dr. Hayes guided his students through additional case studies in digital governance, highlighting successful strategies, lessons learned, and implications for the future of e-government.

"As you explore case studies in digital governance," Dr. Hayes concluded, "consider the diverse approaches governments take to harness technology for the benefit of citizens. By learning from each other's experiences, we can accelerate the pace of digital transformation and create more responsive, inclusive, and effective governance for the digital age."

The students left the lecture hall, inspired by the innovative solutions and transformative potential of digital governance initiatives. Dr. Hayes watched them go, feeling a sense of optimism for the future of governance in the digital era.

10

Chapter 10: Public Administration and Social Equity

Defining Social Equity in Public Administration

Dr. Robert Hayes stood before the class, his demeanor poised yet impassioned as he embarked on a journey to unravel the complexities of social equity in public administration. This segment was pivotal for understanding the role of government in promoting fairness, justice, and inclusivity in society.

"Good morning, class," Dr. Hayes greeted, his voice resonating with authority. "Today, we delve into the fundamental concept of social equity in public administration, exploring its definition, principles, and implications for governance."

He clicked to the first slide, unveiling the title: "Defining Social Equity in Public Administration."

"Social equity," Dr. Hayes began, "refers to the fair and just distribution of resources, opportunities, and privileges within society. In the context of public administration, social equity entails ensuring that all individuals have access to essential services, rights, and opportunities, regardless of their race, ethnicity, gender, socioeconomic status, or other characteristics."

As he spoke, images of diverse communities, inclusive policies, and equitable access to services filled the screen, illustrating the vision of a society where every individual can thrive and succeed.

"The first aspect we must consider is understanding the importance of social equity in public administration," Dr. Hayes continued. "Social equity is a cornerstone of democratic governance, reflecting the principles of fairness, justice, and inclusivity that underpin our society. It requires governments to actively address disparities, systemic inequalities, and barriers to opportunity to ensure that all citizens can fully participate in civic life and enjoy a decent quality of life."

A hand shot up from a student named Emily. "How does social equity differ from equality?"

"Social equity differs from equality in that it recognizes and addresses the unequal distribution of resources and opportunities in society," Dr. Hayes replied. "While equality seeks to treat everyone the same, regardless of their circumstances, social equity acknowledges that individuals may require different levels of support or intervention to achieve equitable outcomes. It involves identifying and rectifying systemic barriers and injustices to create a level playing field for all citizens."

He clicked to the next slide, which read: "Principles of Social Equity."

"The next aspect is understanding the principles of social equity," Dr. Hayes explained. "These principles include fairness, inclusivity, diversity, accessibility, and accountability. Governments must uphold these principles in their policies, programs, and decision-making processes to promote social equity and ensure that no one is left behind."

A student named Marcus raised his hand. "What are some examples of policies that promote social equity?"

"Examples of policies that promote social equity include affirmative action programs, anti-discrimination laws, affordable housing initiatives, healthcare access programs, and educational equity policies," Dr. Hayes replied. "These policies aim to address historical injustices, systemic inequalities, and barriers to opportunity to create a more just and inclusive society for all."

He clicked to the next slide, which displayed the phrase: "Challenges and Opportunities."

"The final aspect we'll explore is the challenges and opportunities of advancing social equity in public administration," Dr. Hayes said. "While promoting social equity presents challenges such as political resistance, resource constraints, and entrenched inequalities, it also offers opportunities to build stronger, more resilient communities, foster social cohesion, and unlock the full potential of all citizens."

As the lecture continued, Dr. Hayes guided his students through examples of social equity initiatives in public administration, highlighting successful strategies, emerging trends, and ongoing challenges in advancing equity and justice in society.

"As you explore social equity in public administration," Dr. Hayes concluded, "consider the profound impact government policies and programs can have on shaping the social fabric of our society. By prioritizing social equity, governments can uphold the values of fairness, justice, and inclusivity and create a more prosperous and equitable future for all."

The students left the lecture hall, contemplative of the principles and challenges of social equity in public administration. Dr. Hayes watched them go, feeling a sense of urgency to inspire them to champion equity and justice in their future roles as public servants.

Policies for Promoting Social Equity

Dr. Robert Hayes, his passion palpable, continued his lecture on social equity in public administration, now delving into the policies that serve as vehicles for promoting fairness and justice in society. This segment was crucial for understanding the tangible actions governments take to address systemic inequalities and ensure equal opportunities for all citizens.

"Good morning, class," Dr. Hayes greeted, his voice brimming with enthusiasm. "Today, we explore the policies that governments implement to promote social equity, examining their design, implementation, and impact on fostering inclusive and just societies."

He clicked to the first slide, unveiling the title: "Policies for Promoting Social Equity."

"Policies for promoting social equity," Dr. Hayes began, "are designed to address systemic disparities, remove barriers to opportunity, and empower marginalized communities to fully participate in society. These policies play a vital role in advancing fairness, justice, and inclusivity in public administration."

As he spoke, images of anti-discrimination laws, affirmative action programs, and social welfare initiatives filled the screen, illustrating the breadth and diversity of policies aimed at promoting social equity.

"The first aspect we must consider is understanding the design of policies for social equity," Dr. Hayes continued. "Effective policies for social equity are grounded in principles of fairness, inclusivity, and accountability. They are targeted, evidence-based, and responsive to the needs of disadvantaged populations, addressing root causes of inequality and promoting pathways to opportunity."

A hand shot up from a student named Emily. "Can you provide examples of policies for promoting social equity?"

"Of course," Dr. Hayes replied. "Examples of policies for promoting social equity include affirmative action programs, which seek to redress historical injustices and increase representation of underrepresented groups in education, employment, and government. Other examples include anti-discrimination laws, minimum wage legislation, affordable housing initiatives, and healthcare access programs, all of which aim to level the playing field and create a more just and inclusive society."

He clicked to the next slide, which read: "Implementation Challenges."

"The next aspect is understanding the challenges of implementing policies for social equity," Dr. Hayes explained. "While policies for social equity are well-intentioned, their implementation often faces challenges such as political opposition, resource constraints, bureaucratic inertia, and resistance from vested interests. Overcoming these challenges requires strong leadership, effective governance structures, and collaborative partnerships with stakeholders."

A student named Marcus raised his hand. "How do governments measure the impact of social equity policies?"

"Governments measure the impact of social equity policies through various metrics, such as access to services, income inequality, educational attainment, and social mobility," Dr. Hayes replied. "They conduct evaluations, collect data, and engage with communities to assess the effectiveness of policies and identify areas for improvement. By tracking progress and outcomes, governments can refine their policies and ensure they are achieving their intended objectives."

He clicked to the next slide, which displayed the phrase: "Building Inclusive Societies."

"The final aspect we'll explore is the role of policies for promoting social equity in building inclusive societies," Dr. Hayes said. "These policies are not just about addressing inequalities; they are about fostering a sense of belonging, dignity, and respect for all individuals, regardless of their background or circumstances. By prioritizing social equity, governments can create a more cohesive, resilient, and prosperous society for all."

As the lecture continued, Dr. Hayes guided his students through examples of policies for promoting social equity, highlighting their design, implementation challenges, and potential impact on fostering inclusive and just societies.

"As you explore policies for promoting social equity," Dr. Hayes concluded, "consider the transformative power of government action in addressing systemic injustices and creating opportunities for all citizens to thrive. By championing social equity, governments can build a more equitable and sustainable future for generations to come."

The students left the lecture hall, inspired by the potential of policies to promote fairness and justice in society. Dr. Hayes watched them go, feeling a sense of optimism for the future of governance in creating a more inclusive and just world.

Addressing Inequities in Public Service Delivery

Dr. Robert Hayes, his expression earnest, transitioned seamlessly into the next segment of his lecture, where he delved into the critical task of addressing inequities in public service delivery. This aspect was fundamental for understanding how governments strive to ensure equal access to essential services for all citizens, regardless of their backgrounds or circumstances.

"Good morning, class," Dr. Hayes greeted, his voice tinged with determination. "Today, we explore the imperative of addressing inequities in public service delivery, examining the challenges, strategies, and innovations governments employ to ensure that all citizens have equal access to essential services."

He clicked to the first slide, unveiling the title: "Addressing Inequities in Public Service Delivery."

"Addressing inequities in public service delivery," Dr. Hayes began, "requires governments to identify disparities in access, quality, and outcomes across different populations and regions. It involves implementing targeted interventions, investing in underserved communities, and redesigning service delivery models to prioritize equity and inclusion."

As he spoke, images of diverse communities, healthcare facilities, and educational institutions filled the screen, illustrating the breadth and depth of public services that governments strive to make accessible to all citizens.

"The first aspect we must consider is understanding the

scope of inequities in public service delivery," Dr. Hayes continued. "Inequities can manifest in various forms, including disparities in access to healthcare, education, transportation, housing, and social services. These inequities disproportionately affect marginalized communities, exacerbating social disparities and perpetuating cycles of poverty and exclusion."

A hand shot up from a student named Emily. "How do governments identify and measure inequities in public service delivery?"

"Governments identify and measure inequities in public service delivery through data analysis, community consultations, and equity impact assessments," Dr. Hayes replied. "They collect demographic data, conduct surveys, and engage with stakeholders to identify disparities in access, utilization, and outcomes of public services. By understanding the root causes of inequities, governments can develop targeted interventions and allocate resources effectively to address disparities and promote social equity."

He clicked to the next slide, which read: "Strategies for Promoting Equity."

"The next aspect is understanding the strategies for promoting equity in public service delivery," Dr. Hayes explained. "These strategies include expanding access to essential services in underserved areas, tailoring services to meet the needs of diverse populations, implementing affirmative action programs to address historical injustices, and fostering partnerships with community organizations to ensure that services are responsive to local needs."

A student named Marcus raised his hand. "What are some examples of initiatives that address inequities in public service delivery?"

"Examples of initiatives that address inequities in public service delivery include community health clinics in under-served neighborhoods, school lunch programs for low-income students, transportation subsidies for rural communities, and affordable housing initiatives for marginalized populations," Dr. Hayes replied. "These initiatives aim to reduce barriers to access, improve service quality, and promote social inclusion for all citizens."

He clicked to the next slide, which displayed the phrase: "Building Inclusive Communities."

"The final aspect we'll explore is the role of addressing inequities in public service delivery in building inclusive communities," Dr. Hayes said. "By ensuring equal access to essential services, governments can promote social cohesion, economic opportunity, and well-being for all citizens, contributing to the development of thriving, resilient, and inclusive communities."

As the lecture continued, Dr. Hayes guided his students through examples of initiatives aimed at addressing inequities in public service delivery, highlighting their impact on promoting social equity and fostering inclusive societies.

"As you explore strategies for promoting equity in public service delivery," Dr. Hayes concluded, "consider the profound impact these initiatives can have on improving the lives of marginalized communities and creating a more just and inclusive society for all. By prioritizing equity in service delivery, governments can fulfill their obligation to ensure that every citizen has the opportunity to thrive."

The students left the lecture hall, inspired by the transformative potential of addressing inequities in public service delivery. Dr. Hayes watched them go, feeling a sense of purpose in equipping them with the knowledge and tools to champion equity and justice in their future roles as public servants.

Role of Public Administrators in Advancing Equity

Dr. Robert Hayes, his tone reflective yet resolute, shifted the focus of his lecture to the pivotal role of public administrators in advancing equity within society. This aspect was crucial for understanding how government officials serve as catalysts for change, working tirelessly to dismantle systemic barriers and foster inclusivity in public service delivery.

"Good morning, class," Dr. Hayes greeted, his voice conveying a sense of purpose. "Today, we explore the indispensable role of public administrators in advancing equity, examining their responsibilities, challenges, and opportunities in promoting fairness and justice within society."

He clicked to the first slide, unveiling the title: "Role of Public Administrators in Advancing Equity."

"The role of public administrators in advancing equity," Dr. Hayes began, "is multifaceted and far-reaching. It encompasses a range of responsibilities, from policymaking and program implementation to community engagement and advocacy. Public administrators serve as stewards of equity, striving to ensure that government policies and programs are inclusive, responsive, and equitable for all citizens."

As he spoke, images of diverse public administrators engaging with communities, leading initiatives, and advocating for equity filled the screen, illustrating the breadth and depth of their impact on promoting social justice.

"The first aspect we must consider is understanding the

responsibilities of public administrators in advancing equity," Dr. Hayes continued. "Public administrators are responsible for designing and implementing policies and programs that promote social equity, addressing inequities in public service delivery, and fostering partnerships with community organizations to ensure that government initiatives are responsive to local needs."

A hand shot up from a student named Emily. "What are some challenges public administrators face in advancing equity?"

"Public administrators face numerous challenges in advancing equity, including limited resources, bureaucratic inertia, political resistance, and entrenched inequalities," Dr. Hayes replied. "They must navigate complex political environments, engage with diverse stakeholders, and address competing interests to advance equity effectively. Overcoming these challenges requires strong leadership, strategic planning, and a commitment to collaboration and innovation."

He clicked to the next slide, which read: "Opportunities for Impact."

"The next aspect is understanding the opportunities for impact that public administrators have in advancing equity," Dr. Hayes explained. "Public administrators can leverage their positions to advocate for policy reforms, promote diversity and inclusion within government agencies, and build coalitions with community organizations to address systemic injustices. By championing equity in their roles, public administrators can drive positive change and create more just and inclusive societies."

A student named Marcus raised his hand. "How can public administrators engage with communities to advance equity?"

"Public administrators can engage with communities through various means, such as conducting outreach events, soliciting feedback through public hearings, and collaborating with community organizations on policy development and implementation," Dr. Hayes replied. "By listening to the voices of those most affected by inequities, public administrators can better understand community needs, priorities, and aspirations, and tailor government initiatives to address them effectively."

He clicked to the next slide, which displayed the phrase: "Building Equitable Institutions."

"The final aspect we'll explore is the role of public administrators in building equitable institutions," Dr. Hayes said. "Equitable institutions are those that prioritize fairness, justice, and inclusivity in their policies, practices, and culture. Public administrators play a critical role in fostering a culture of equity within government agencies, promoting diversity in hiring and decision-making, and ensuring that institutional processes are transparent, accountable, and responsive to the needs of all citizens."

As the lecture continued, Dr. Hayes guided his students through examples of public administrators leading initiatives to advance equity, highlighting their impact on promoting social justice and inclusivity within society.

"As you explore the role of public administrators in advancing equity," Dr. Hayes concluded, "consider the transformative power of their leadership in creating a more just, equitable, and inclusive society for all. By embracing their responsibilities and opportunities for impact, public administrators can be catalysts for positive change and champions of social justice within government and beyond."

The students left the lecture hall, inspired by the potential of public administrators to drive meaningful progress in advancing equity. Dr. Hayes watched them go, feeling a sense of pride in their eagerness to tackle the challenges of building a more just and equitable world.

Case Studies in Social Equity

Dr. Robert Hayes, his demeanor now filled with anticipation, embarked on the final segment of his lecture, where he would delve into real-world case studies showcasing successful initiatives in promoting social equity. This aspect was pivotal for bridging theory with practice, allowing students to glean insights from practical examples and apply them to their future roles as public administrators.

"Good morning, class," Dr. Hayes greeted, his voice resonating with enthusiasm. "Today, we conclude our exploration of social equity in public administration by examining case studies that demonstrate innovative and effective strategies for promoting fairness, justice, and inclusion within society."

He clicked to the first slide, unveiling the title: "Case Studies in Social Equity."

"Case studies in social equity," Dr. Hayes began, "provide valuable insights into the practical application of equity principles in government policies, programs, and practices. By analyzing real-world examples, we can identify key success factors, lessons learned, and opportunities for replication and improvement."

As he spoke, images of diverse communities, government initiatives, and transformative outcomes filled the screen, illustrating the impact of social equity efforts on improving lives and fostering inclusive societies.

"The first case study we'll explore is the Community Health Equity Initiative," Dr. Hayes continued. "This initiative, implemented by the Department of Health in collaboration with local community organizations, aimed to address health disparities in underserved neighborhoods by increasing access to affordable healthcare services, promoting preventive care, and addressing social determinants of health."

He clicked to the next slide, which displayed images of community health clinics, wellness programs, and outreach events.

"The Community Health Equity Initiative leveraged partnerships with community organizations to establish neighborhood health clinics, provide culturally competent care, and offer health education and outreach programs tailored to the needs of local residents," Dr. Hayes explained. "By addressing social determinants of health, such as poverty, housing insecurity, and food insecurity, the initiative improved health outcomes, reduced healthcare disparities, and empowered communities to take control of their health and well-being."

A hand shot up from a student named Emily. "What were some key factors contributing to the success of the initiative?"

"Key factors contributing to the success of the Community Health Equity Initiative included community engagement, collaborative partnerships, culturally responsive care, and a holistic approach to addressing health disparities," Dr. Hayes replied. "By involving community members in the planning, implementation, and evaluation of the initiative, and tailoring services to meet their unique needs and preferences, the initiative was able to build trust, increase access to care, and achieve meaningful improvements in health outcomes."

He clicked to the next slide, which read: "Lessons Learned."

"The next case study we'll examine is the Equity in Education Program," Dr. Hayes said. "This program, implemented by the Department of Education in partnership with local school districts, aimed to reduce achievement gaps and improve educational outcomes for students from disadvantaged backgrounds."

As the lecture continued, Dr. Hayes guided his students through a series of case studies showcasing successful initiatives in promoting social equity, highlighting their impact on addressing systemic disparities and fostering inclusive communities.

"As you explore these case studies," Dr. Hayes concluded, "consider the valuable lessons they offer for advancing social equity in public administration. By learning from successful examples and applying best practices, we can build a more just, equitable, and inclusive society for all."

The students left the lecture hall, inspired by the transformative potential of case studies in promoting social equity. Dr. Hayes watched them go, feeling a sense of hope for the future as they embarked on their journey to become agents of change in the pursuit of social justice.

Evaluating Equity Outcomes

Dr. Robert Hayes, his demeanor now focused and determined, shifted the discussion to the critical task of evaluating equity outcomes. This aspect was essential for ensuring accountability, measuring progress, and refining strategies to advance social justice within society.

"Good morning, class," Dr. Hayes greeted, his voice infused

with purpose. "Today, we conclude our examination of social equity in public administration by exploring the importance of evaluating equity outcomes, assessing the effectiveness of policies and programs in promoting fairness, justice, and inclusion."

He clicked to the first slide, unveiling the title: "Evaluating Equity Outcomes."

"Evaluating equity outcomes," Dr. Hayes began, "is essential for determining whether government initiatives are achieving their intended objectives, addressing disparities, and improving outcomes for marginalized communities. It involves collecting and analyzing data, measuring impact, and assessing the effectiveness of interventions in promoting social equity."

As he spoke, images of data analytics, performance metrics, and impact assessments filled the screen, illustrating the tools and methodologies used to evaluate equity outcomes in public administration.

"The first aspect we must consider is understanding the importance of evaluating equity outcomes," Dr. Hayes continued. "Evaluation allows us to assess the effectiveness of policies and programs in advancing social equity, identify areas for improvement, and allocate resources strategically to address disparities. By measuring progress and outcomes, we can ensure that government initiatives are responsive to the needs of all citizens and contribute to building more just and inclusive societies."

A hand shot up from a student named Emily. "How do governments collect data for evaluating equity outcomes?"

"Governments collect data for evaluating equity outcomes through various means, such as surveys, administrative records, focus groups, and community consultations," Dr. Hayes replied. "They gather demographic information, assess service utilization, and measure outcomes across different population groups to identify disparities and assess the impact of policies and programs. By disaggregating data by race, ethnicity, gender, income, and other relevant factors, governments can identify inequities and tailor interventions to address them effectively."

He clicked to the next slide, which read: "Measuring Impact."

"The next aspect is understanding how to measure the impact of equity initiatives," Dr. Hayes explained. "Measuring impact involves assessing changes in outcomes, such as access to services, quality of life, and social indicators, as a result of government interventions. It requires establishing clear indicators, setting targets, and tracking progress over time to determine whether equity objectives are being achieved."

A student named Marcus raised his hand. "What are some challenges in evaluating equity outcomes?"

"Challenges in evaluating equity outcomes include data limitations, measurement issues, interpretation biases, and resource constraints," Dr. Hayes replied. "Collecting reliable data, accounting for confounding factors, and attributing changes in outcomes to specific interventions can be complex and nuanced. Moreover, ensuring that evaluation findings are used to inform policy decisions and improve programs requires strong leadership, institutional support, and a commitment to evidence-based decision-making."

He clicked to the next slide, which displayed the phrase: "Improving Equity Strategies."

"The final aspect we'll explore is using evaluation findings to improve equity strategies," Dr. Hayes said. "Evaluation is not just about assessing past performance; it's about using evidence to inform future actions and enhance the effectiveness of equity initiatives. By learning from successes and failures, governments can refine their strategies, innovate new approaches, and continuously strive to advance social justice and inclusion within society."

As the lecture continued, Dr. Hayes guided his students through examples of evaluation methods and best practices in assessing equity outcomes, highlighting their importance in driving evidence-based policy and decision-making.

"As you explore the role of evaluation in promoting social equity," Dr. Hayes concluded, "consider the transformative power of data and evidence in guiding government action and shaping a more just and inclusive future for all. By prioritizing evaluation in our efforts to advance equity, we can ensure that government initiatives are responsive, accountable, and effective in addressing the needs of all citizens."

The students left the lecture hall, inspired by the potential of evaluation to drive meaningful change in promoting social equity. Dr. Hayes watched them go, feeling a sense of optimism for the future as they embarked on their journey to apply their knowledge and skills in advancing justice and fairness within society.

Chapter 11: Intergovernmental Relations and Federalism

Structure of Federal Systems

Dr. Robert Hayes, his demeanor poised and authoritative, commenced the exploration of the structural intricacies of federal systems, a cornerstone of modern governance. This subpoint delved into the organizational framework of federalism, elucidating the division of powers and responsibilities between central and regional governments.

"Good morning, class," Dr. Hayes greeted, his voice resonating with scholarly wisdom. "Today, we delve into the structural foundations of federal systems, examining the organizational architecture that underpins the distribution of powers and functions among different levels of government."

He clicked to the first slide, unveiling the title: "Structure of Federal Systems."

"The structure of federal systems," Dr. Hayes began, "is

characterized by a dual government framework, comprising a central authority and constituent units with autonomous powers. This organizational arrangement allows for the division of responsibilities, with certain powers vested in the central government, others in regional or state governments, and some shared between them."

As he spoke, images of legislative chambers, administrative agencies, and constitutional documents filled the screen, illustrating the complex web of institutions and mechanisms that govern federal systems.

"The first aspect we must consider is the distribution of powers in federal systems," Dr. Hayes continued. "Federal systems typically allocate powers through written constitutions, which delineate the authority of the central government, the powers reserved to states or provinces, and the areas of concurrent jurisdiction where both levels of government may legislate."

A hand shot up from a student named Emily. "How do federal systems balance centralization and decentralization of power?"

"Federal systems balance centralization and decentralization through mechanisms such as enumerated powers, which specify the authority of the central government, and residual powers, which are reserved to the states or provinces," Dr. Hayes replied. "Additionally, federal systems may establish mechanisms for intergovernmental cooperation and dispute resolution to facilitate coordination and collaboration between different levels of government."

He clicked to the next slide, which read: "Types of Federalism."

"The next aspect is understanding the different types of

federalism," Dr. Hayes explained. "Federal systems can vary in their degree of centralization and decentralization, ranging from cooperative federalism, where the central and state governments work closely together, to dual federalism, where the powers of the central and state governments are more clearly delineated and separate."

A student named Marcus raised his hand. "How do federal systems evolve over time?"

"Federal systems can evolve over time in response to changing political, social, and economic dynamics," Dr. Hayes replied. "They may experience shifts in the balance of power between central and state governments, changes in the scope and nature of intergovernmental relations, and reforms to address emerging challenges or promote greater efficiency and effectiveness in governance."

He clicked to the next slide, which displayed the phrase: "Challenges in Federal Systems."

"The final aspect we'll explore is the challenges inherent in federal systems," Dr. Hayes said. "While federalism offers many benefits, such as promoting diversity, accommodating regional differences, and fostering experimentation and innovation, it also presents challenges, such as jurisdictional conflicts, fiscal disparities, and coordination issues. Navigating these challenges requires effective mechanisms for intergovernmental cooperation, conflict resolution, and policy coordination."

As the lecture continued, Dr. Hayes guided his students through the complexities of federal systems, providing insights into their structural foundations and dynamic evolution.

"As you explore the structure of federal systems," Dr. Hayes concluded, "consider the delicate balance between centralization and decentralization, and the importance of effective mechanisms for cooperation and coordination in ensuring the success of federal governance. By understanding these dynamics, we can better navigate the complexities of modern governance and build more resilient and responsive systems of government."

The students left the lecture hall, their minds buzzing with newfound understanding of the organizational intricacies of federalism. Dr. Hayes watched them go, confident in their ability to grasp the complexities of federal systems and apply their knowledge to the challenges of public administration in the real world.

Intergovernmental Coordination and Cooperation

Dr. Robert Hayes, his demeanor exuding scholarly authority, delved deeper into the intricate dynamics of intergovernmental coordination and cooperation, essential for navigating the complexities of federal systems. This subpoint explored the mechanisms through which governments at different levels collaborate to address shared challenges and deliver public services effectively.

"Good morning, class," Dr. Hayes greeted, his voice resonating with gravitas. "Today, we continue our exploration of intergovernmental relations and federalism by examining the critical importance of coordination and cooperation among different levels of government in achieving common objectives."

He clicked to the first slide, unveiling the title: "Intergovernmental Coordination and Cooperation."

"Intergovernmental coordination and cooperation," Dr. Hayes began, "are essential for ensuring the smooth functioning of federal systems, facilitating the delivery of public services, and addressing complex societal challenges that transcend jurisdictional boundaries."

As he spoke, images of government officials collaborating in meetings, signing agreements, and working together on joint projects filled the screen, illustrating the diverse ways in which intergovernmental cooperation manifests in practice.

"The first aspect we must consider is the need for effective mechanisms of coordination," Dr. Hayes continued. "Coordination involves the alignment of policies, programs, and actions across different levels of government to achieve common goals and avoid duplication or fragmentation of efforts."

A hand shot up from a student named Emily. "What are some examples of intergovernmental coordination in action?"

"Examples of intergovernmental coordination include joint planning processes for infrastructure projects, shared data-sharing agreements for public health surveillance, and interagency task forces for emergency response," Dr. Hayes replied. "These mechanisms allow governments to pool resources, leverage expertise, and coordinate activities to address complex challenges more effectively than they could individually."

He clicked to the next slide, which read: "Interagency Cooperation."

"The next aspect is understanding the importance of interagency cooperation," Dr. Hayes explained. "Interagency cooperation involves collaboration among different government agencies and departments at the same level of government to achieve common objectives. It requires communication, information-sharing, and joint decision-making to ensure that policies and programs are implemented coherently and efficiently."

A student named Marcus raised his hand. "How do governments foster interagency cooperation?"

"Governments foster interagency cooperation through mechanisms such as interagency councils, working groups, and cross-functional teams," Dr. Hayes replied. "These structures provide forums for agencies to exchange information, coordinate activities, and resolve conflicts or differences in approach. Additionally, governments may incentivize cooperation through performance metrics, funding mechanisms, and leadership directives to prioritize collaboration and shared goals."

He clicked to the next slide, which displayed the phrase: "Challenges in Intergovernmental Cooperation."

"The final aspect we'll explore is the challenges inherent in intergovernmental cooperation," Dr. Hayes said. "While cooperation offers many benefits, such as leveraging resources, sharing expertise, and achieving economies of scale, it also presents challenges, such as competing priorities, divergent interests, and bureaucratic inertia. Overcoming these challenges requires effective leadership, communication, and negotiation skills to build consensus and foster a culture of collaboration."

As the lecture continued, Dr. Hayes guided his students through examples of successful intergovernmental coordination and cooperation, highlighting their importance in addressing complex societal challenges and delivering public services efficiently.

"As you explore the dynamics of intergovernmental coordination and cooperation," Dr. Hayes concluded, "consider the critical role these mechanisms play in achieving common objectives and advancing the public interest. By fostering collaboration and coordination among different levels of government, we can build more effective and responsive systems of governance that meet the needs of all citizens."

The students left the lecture hall, their minds buzzing with newfound understanding of the intricate dance of cooperation among governments. Dr. Hayes watched them go, confident in their ability to grasp the complexities of intergovernmental relations and apply their knowledge to the challenges of public administration in the real world.

Fiscal Federalism and Resource Allocation

Dr. Robert Hayes, his presence commanding the room, delved into the intricate dynamics of fiscal federalism and resource allocation, two fundamental aspects of intergovernmental relations. This subpoint elucidated the mechanisms through which governments manage financial resources and distribute funds to address the needs of citizens within federal systems.

"Good morning, class," Dr. Hayes greeted, his voice projecting authority and knowledge. "Today, we continue our exploration of intergovernmental relations and federalism by delving into the complex realm of fiscal federalism and resource allocation."

He clicked to the first slide, unveiling the title: "Fiscal Federalism and Resource Allocation."

"Fiscal federalism," Dr. Hayes began, "refers to the distribution of financial resources and responsibilities among different levels of government within federal systems. It encompasses revenue generation, taxation, intergovernmental transfers, and expenditure management, all of which play a crucial role in determining the capacity of governments to deliver public services and meet the needs of citizens."

As he spoke, images of budget documents, tax forms, and revenue streams filled the screen, illustrating the diverse ways in which financial resources flow through federal systems.

"The first aspect we must consider is the role of revenue generation and taxation," Dr. Hayes continued. "Revenue generation involves the collection of funds through various sources, such as taxes, fees, and charges, to finance government activities and programs. Taxation policies, in particular, play a significant role in shaping the distribution of financial resources and the fiscal capacities of different levels of government."

A hand shot up from a student named Emily. "How do governments balance the need for revenue with concerns about tax fairness and economic efficiency?"

"Balancing the need for revenue with concerns about tax fairness and economic efficiency requires governments to consider factors such as tax incidence, progressivity, and administrative simplicity," Dr. Hayes replied. "They must design tax policies that are equitable, efficient, and conducive to economic growth while also ensuring that the burden of taxation is distributed fairly among citizens and businesses."

He clicked to the next slide, which read: "Intergovernmental Transfers."

"The next aspect is understanding the role of intergovernmental transfers," Dr. Hayes explained. "Intergovernmental transfers involve the flow of funds from one level of government to another, typically to address fiscal disparities, promote equalization, or support specific policy objectives. These transfers can take various forms, including grants, subsidies, and revenue-sharing arrangements."

A student named Marcus raised his hand. "How do governments determine the allocation of intergovernmental transfers?"

"Governments determine the allocation of intergovernmental transfers based on factors such as fiscal capacity, revenue needs, policy priorities, and performance indicators," Dr. Hayes replied. "They may use formulas, criteria, or negotiations to allocate funds equitably and transparently, ensuring that resources are directed to areas of greatest need or strategic importance."

He clicked to the next slide, which displayed the phrase: "Challenges in Fiscal Federalism."

"The final aspect we'll explore is the challenges inherent in fiscal federalism," Dr. Hayes said. "While fiscal federalism offers many benefits, such as promoting fiscal autonomy, fostering competition, and enabling experimentation, it also presents challenges, such as vertical fiscal imbalances, overlapping responsibilities, and budgetary constraints. Overcoming these challenges requires effective mechanisms for coordination, cooperation, and fiscal discipline to ensure that resources are allocated efficiently and equitably."

As the lecture continued, Dr. Hayes guided his students through examples of fiscal federalism in practice, highlighting its impact on government revenues, expenditures, and service delivery.

"As you explore the dynamics of fiscal federalism and resource allocation," Dr. Hayes concluded, "consider the importance of sound fiscal management, transparency, and accountability in ensuring that financial resources are used effectively to meet the needs of citizens. By understanding these principles, we can build more resilient and responsive systems of governance that promote economic prosperity and social well-being."

The students left the lecture hall, their minds buzzing with newfound understanding of the intricate interplay of financial resources within federal systems. Dr. Hayes watched them go, confident in their ability to apply their knowledge to the challenges of public administration in the real world.

Legal Frameworks and Jurisdictional Issues

Dr. Robert Hayes, his voice carrying the weight of authority, delved into the complex realm of legal frameworks and jurisdictional issues within federal systems, essential for navigating the intricacies of intergovernmental relations. This subpoint elucidated the legal structures and mechanisms that govern the distribution of powers and resolve conflicts between different levels of government.

"Good morning, class," Dr. Hayes greeted, his tone resonating with scholarly wisdom. "Today, we continue our exploration of intergovernmental relations and federalism by examining the critical role of legal frameworks and jurisdictional issues in shaping the dynamics of federal systems."

He clicked to the first slide, unveiling the title: "Legal Frameworks and Jurisdictional Issues."

"Legal frameworks," Dr. Hayes began, "establish the rules, principles, and procedures that govern the allocation of powers and responsibilities among different levels of government within federal systems. They provide the foundation for inter-governmental cooperation, define the scope of government authority, and ensure that conflicts are resolved in a fair and orderly manner."

As he spoke, images of courtrooms, legislative chambers, and constitutional documents filled the screen, illustrating the diverse ways in which legal frameworks manifest in practice.

"The first aspect we must consider is the division of powers," Dr. Hayes continued. "Federal systems typically allocate powers through written constitutions, which delineate the authority of the central government, the powers reserved to states or provinces, and the areas of concurrent jurisdiction where both levels of government may legislate."

A hand shot up from a student named Emily. "How do legal frameworks address conflicts between central and state governments?"

"Legal frameworks address conflicts between central and state governments through mechanisms such as judicial review, constitutional interpretation, and dispute resolution procedures," Dr. Hayes replied. "Courts play a crucial role in adjudicating disputes, interpreting constitutional provisions, and clarifying the respective powers and responsibilities of different levels of government."

He clicked to the next slide, which read: "Jurisdictional Issues."

"The next aspect is understanding jurisdictional issues," Dr. Hayes explained. "Jurisdictional issues arise when there is ambiguity or overlap in the allocation of powers between different levels of government, leading to conflicts over authority, responsibilities, and decision-making. These issues can arise in various areas, including taxation, regulation, and service delivery."

A student named Marcus raised his hand. "How do governments resolve jurisdictional issues?"

"Governments resolve jurisdictional issues through mechanisms such as intergovernmental agreements, negotiation, and cooperative federalism," Dr. Hayes replied. "They may also seek clarification from courts or establish dispute resolution mechanisms to address conflicts in a timely and effective manner. Ultimately, resolving jurisdictional issues requires a commitment to dialogue, collaboration, and compromise among all levels of government."

He clicked to the next slide, which displayed the phrase: "Challenges in Intergovernmental Relations."

"The final aspect we'll explore is the challenges inherent in intergovernmental relations," Dr. Hayes said. "While legal frameworks provide the foundation for cooperation and conflict resolution, they also present challenges, such as interpretation issues, enforcement difficulties, and jurisdictional disputes. Overcoming these challenges requires governments to uphold the rule of law, respect constitutional principles, and work together to find mutually acceptable solutions to complex jurisdictional issues."

As the lecture continued, Dr. Hayes guided his students through examples of legal frameworks and jurisdictional issues in practice, highlighting their impact on governance, policy, and the rule of law.

"As you explore the dynamics of legal frameworks and jurisdictional issues," Dr. Hayes concluded, "consider the importance of clarity, consistency, and collaboration in ensuring effective intergovernmental relations. By upholding the principles of federalism and the rule of law, we can build more resilient and responsive systems of governance that serve the needs of all citizens."

The students left the lecture hall, their minds buzzing with newfound understanding of the legal underpinnings of federal systems. Dr. Hayes watched them go, confident in their ability to apply their knowledge to the challenges of public administration in the real world.

Challenges in Intergovernmental Relations

Dr. Robert Hayes, his voice resonating with scholarly authority, delved into the myriad challenges inherent in intergovernmental relations within federal systems, essential for understanding the complexities of modern governance. This subpoint illuminated the obstacles that governments face in coordinating their activities, resolving conflicts, and delivering public services effectively across multiple levels of authority.

"Good morning, class," Dr. Hayes greeted, his tone conveying a sense of gravitas. "Today, we confront the challenges that beset intergovernmental relations within federal systems, shedding light on the complexities that governments must navigate in their pursuit of cooperative governance."

He clicked to the first slide, unveiling the title: "Challenges in Intergovernmental Relations."

"Intergovernmental relations," Dr. Hayes began, "are fraught with a multitude of challenges that stem from the inherent tensions between centralization and decentralization, the distribution of powers, and the diversity of interests among different levels of government."

As he spoke, images of legislative gridlock, jurisdictional

disputes, and bureaucratic inefficiencies filled the screen, illustrating the multifaceted nature of the challenges faced by governments in their efforts to collaborate effectively.

"The first challenge we must confront is the issue of vertical fiscal imbalances," Dr. Hayes continued. "Vertical fiscal imbalances occur when there is a misalignment between revenue-raising powers and expenditure responsibilities among different levels of government. This imbalance can lead to disparities in fiscal capacity, fiscal stress, and inequities in the provision of public services."

A hand shot up from a student named Emily. "How do governments address vertical fiscal imbalances?"

"Governments address vertical fiscal imbalances through mechanisms such as intergovernmental transfers, revenue-sharing arrangements, and fiscal equalization programs," Dr. Hayes replied. "These mechanisms aim to redistribute resources from financially stronger to weaker governments, promote fiscal equity, and ensure that all citizens have access to essential public services."

He clicked to the next slide, which read: "Coordination Challenges."

"The next challenge is coordination challenges," Dr. Hayes explained. "Coordination challenges arise when there is a lack of alignment, cooperation, or communication among different levels of government, leading to inefficiencies, duplications, and gaps in service delivery. These challenges can stem from differences in priorities, mandates, or organizational cultures among government agencies."

A student named Marcus raised his hand. "How do governments overcome coordination challenges?"

"Governments overcome coordination challenges through

mechanisms such as interagency cooperation, joint planning processes, and information-sharing agreements," Dr. Hayes replied. "They may also establish coordinating bodies, task forces, or working groups to facilitate collaboration and streamline decision-making across different levels of government. By fostering a culture of cooperation and communication, governments can enhance the effectiveness and efficiency of their intergovernmental relations."

He clicked to the next slide, which displayed the phrase: "Political Conflicts."

"The final challenge we'll explore is political conflicts," Dr. Hayes said. "Political conflicts arise when there are divergent interests, priorities, or ideologies among different levels of government, leading to tensions, gridlock, or policy stalemates. These conflicts can hinder cooperation, impede progress, and undermine the effectiveness of intergovernmental relations."

As the lecture continued, Dr. Hayes guided his students through examples of challenges in intergovernmental relations, highlighting their impact on governance, policy, and service delivery.

"As you explore the challenges in intergovernmental relations," Dr. Hayes concluded, "consider the importance of dialogue, negotiation, and compromise in overcoming differences and building consensus among different levels of government. By addressing these challenges head-on, we can forge stronger partnerships and achieve greater outcomes for the citizens we serve."

The students left the lecture hall, their minds buzzing with newfound understanding of the obstacles that governments face in their pursuit of cooperative governance. Dr. Hayes watched them go, confident in their ability to apply their knowledge to the challenges of public administration in the real world.

Case Studies in Federalism

Dr. Robert Hayes, his voice a beacon of knowledge and experience, delved into compelling case studies that illuminated the intricacies of federalism and intergovernmental relations. This subpoint provided real-world examples of how governments navigate the challenges and opportunities presented by federal systems, offering valuable insights into the complexities of modern governance.

"Good morning, class," Dr. Hayes greeted, his demeanor exuding scholarly authority. "Today, we embark on a journey through fascinating case studies that showcase the diverse manifestations of federalism and intergovernmental relations in practice."

He clicked to the first slide, unveiling the title: "Case Studies in Federalism."

"These case studies offer valuable insights into how governments around the world grapple with the complexities of federal systems, address jurisdictional conflicts, and foster cooperation among different levels of authority," Dr. Hayes explained.

As he spoke, images of government leaders, legislative chambers, and policy documents filled the screen, each representing a unique example of federalism in action.

"The first case study we'll explore is the Canadian Federation," Dr. Hayes began. "Canada's federal system divides powers between the central government and ten provinces, each with its own distinct responsibilities and policy priorities. Over the years, Canada has navigated challenges such as linguistic and cultural diversity, regional disparities, and tensions between federal and provincial governments."

A hand shot up from a student named Emily. "How does Canada manage its intergovernmental relations?"

"Canada manages its intergovernmental relations through mechanisms such as the Council of the Federation, which brings together provincial and territorial leaders to discuss common challenges and priorities," Dr. Hayes replied. "They also use collaborative processes such as intergovernmental conferences, joint committees, and bilateral agreements to address jurisdictional issues and coordinate policy efforts."

He clicked to the next slide, which read: "The European Union."

"The next case study is the European Union," Dr. Hayes continued. "The EU is a unique example of supranational federalism, where member states pool their sovereignty to address common challenges such as economic integration, security cooperation, and environmental protection. The EU's complex system of governance involves multiple levels of authority, including the European Commission, the European Parliament, and the Council of the European Union."

A student named Marcus raised his hand. "What are some challenges faced by the EU in managing its federal system?"

"Some challenges faced by the EU include tensions between member states over issues such as sovereignty, migration, and economic policy," Dr. Hayes replied. "There are also concerns about democratic legitimacy, accountability, and the balance of power between EU institutions and national governments. Despite these challenges, the EU has demonstrated resilience and adaptability in its efforts to promote cooperation and integration among its member states."

He clicked to the next slide, which displayed the phrase: "The United States."

"The final case study is the United States," Dr. Hayes said. "The US federal system divides powers between the federal government and fifty states, each with its own constitution, laws, and policy prerogatives. Throughout its history, the US has grappled with issues such as states' rights, racial segregation, and the balance of power between the federal government and the states."

As the lecture continued, Dr. Hayes guided his students through a series of captivating case studies, each offering valuable lessons and insights into the complexities of federalism and intergovernmental relations.

"As you explore these case studies," Dr. Hayes concluded, "consider the diverse ways in which governments navigate the challenges and opportunities presented by federal systems. By studying real-world examples, we can gain a deeper understanding of the principles and practices that underpin modern governance."

The students left the lecture hall, their minds enriched by the illuminating case studies presented by Dr. Hayes. Dr. Hayes watched them go, knowing that they had gained valuable insights into the complexities of federalism and intergovernmental relations that would serve them well in their future endeavors.

12

Chapter 12: Public Policy Evaluation and Analysis

Principles of Policy Evaluation

D r. Robert Hayes, a beacon of academic authority, delved into the fundamental principles that underpin the evaluation and analysis of public policies, essential for understanding their effectiveness and impact on society. This subpoint illuminated the methodologies and criteria used to assess the outcomes, efficiency, and equity of government policies, offering valuable insights into the complexities of policymaking in modern governance.

"Good morning, class," Dr. Hayes greeted, his voice carrying the weight of expertise. "Today, we embark on a journey through the principles that guide the evaluation and analysis of public policies, shedding light on the methods and criteria used to assess their effectiveness and impact."

He clicked to the first slide, unveiling the title: "Principles of Policy Evaluation."

"Policy evaluation," Dr. Hayes began, "is the systematic assessment of government policies and programs to determine their outcomes, efficiency, and equity. It involves gathering and analyzing data, measuring performance against predetermined criteria, and making evidence-based recommendations for improvement."

As he spoke, images of data charts, evaluation frameworks, and policy documents filled the screen, each representing a facet of the evaluation process.

"The first principle we must consider is the importance of clarity in defining policy objectives and outcomes," Dr. Hayes continued. "Policy objectives should be clear, specific, and measurable, allowing evaluators to assess whether the policy has achieved its intended goals. By clearly defining objectives, policymakers can focus their efforts on outcomes that matter most to society."

A hand shot up from a student named Emily. "How do policymakers ensure that policy objectives are achievable and realistic?"

"Policymakers ensure that policy objectives are achievable and realistic by conducting thorough research, consulting with stakeholders, and considering feasibility constraints," Dr. Hayes replied. "They may also use pilot programs or pilot studies to test the feasibility of proposed policies before full-scale implementation. By setting achievable and realistic objectives, policymakers can increase the likelihood of policy success and effectiveness."

He clicked to the next slide, which read: "Criteria for Evaluation."

"The next principle is the importance of establishing clear criteria for evaluation," Dr. Hayes explained. "Criteria serve as benchmarks against which policy outcomes are assessed, allowing evaluators to measure performance, identify strengths and weaknesses, and make informed judgments about policy effectiveness. Common criteria for evaluation include efficiency, effectiveness, equity, and sustainability."

A student named Marcus raised his hand. "How do evaluators ensure that criteria are relevant and appropriate for assessing policy outcomes?"

"Evaluators ensure that criteria are relevant and appropriate by consulting with stakeholders, experts, and affected communities," Dr. Hayes replied. "They may also conduct literature reviews, expert interviews, and focus groups to gather input and feedback on the selection of criteria. By involving stakeholders in the evaluation process, evaluators can enhance the validity and credibility of their findings."

He clicked to the next slide, which displayed the phrase: "Data Collection and Analysis."

"The final principle we'll explore is the importance of rigorous data collection and analysis," Dr. Hayes said. "Data collection involves gathering relevant information on policy implementation, outcomes, and impacts, while data analysis involves analyzing and interpreting this information to draw meaningful conclusions about policy effectiveness. Rigorous data collection and analysis are essential for producing credible and reliable evaluation findings."

As the lecture continued, Dr. Hayes guided his students through examples of policy evaluation in practice, highlighting the methods, challenges, and ethical considerations involved in assessing policy outcomes.

"As you explore the principles of policy evaluation," Dr. Hayes concluded, "consider the importance of transparency, rigor, and objectivity in producing credible and actionable evaluation findings. By adhering to these principles, we can ensure that public policies are evidence-based, accountable, and responsive to the needs of society."

The students left the lecture hall, their minds enriched by the principles of policy evaluation presented by Dr. Hayes. Dr. Hayes watched them go, knowing that they had gained valuable insights into the complexities of assessing policy effectiveness and impact.

Methodologies for Policy Analysis

Dr. Robert Hayes, a bastion of scholarly wisdom, delved into the diverse methodologies used to analyze public policies, essential for understanding their underlying mechanisms, effects, and implications. This subpoint illuminated the array of quantitative and qualitative approaches employed by policymakers and analysts to assess the strengths, weaknesses, and unintended consequences of government interventions.

"Good morning, class," Dr. Hayes greeted, his voice resonating with scholarly authority. "Today, we continue our exploration of public policy evaluation and analysis by examining the methodologies used to assess the effectiveness and impact of government policies."

He clicked to the first slide, unveiling the title: "Methodologies for Policy Analysis."

"Policy analysis," Dr. Hayes began, "involves the systematic examination of policy options, alternatives, and outcomes to inform decision-making and improve policy effectiveness. It encompasses a wide range of quantitative and qualitative methods, each offering unique insights into the complex dynamics of policymaking and implementation."

As he spoke, images of data charts, surveys, and policy briefs filled the screen, illustrating the diverse array of methodologies used in policy analysis.

"The first methodology we'll explore is cost-benefit analysis," Dr. Hayes continued. "Cost-benefit analysis involves comparing the costs and benefits of policy alternatives to determine their relative desirability and efficiency. It helps policymakers identify the most cost-effective options for achieving desired outcomes and allocate resources more effectively."

A hand shot up from a student named Emily. "How do policymakers account for intangible costs and benefits in cost-benefit analysis?"

"Policymakers account for intangible costs and benefits in cost-benefit analysis by using techniques such as contingent valuation, stated preference surveys, and willingness-to-pay studies," Dr. Hayes replied. "These methods allow policymakers to estimate the value that individuals place on intangible factors such as environmental quality, health outcomes, and social well-being, enabling them to make more comprehensive and informed decisions."

He clicked to the next slide, which read: "Policy Process Models."

"The next methodology is policy process models," Dr. Hayes explained. "Policy process models provide frameworks for understanding how policies are formulated, adopted, implemented, and evaluated over time. They help analysts identify key actors, institutions, and factors that shape policy outcomes, as well as the dynamics of policy change and implementation."

A student named Marcus raised his hand. "How do policy-makers use policy process models to improve policy effectiveness?"

"Policymakers use policy process models to identify bottlenecks, inefficiencies, and barriers to effective policy implementation," Dr. Hayes replied. "By understanding the underlying dynamics of the policy process, policymakers can anticipate challenges, mitigate risks, and design more responsive and adaptable policy interventions."

He clicked to the next slide, which displayed the phrase: "Qualitative Methods."

"The final methodology we'll explore is qualitative methods," Dr. Hayes said. "Qualitative methods such as case studies, interviews, and focus groups provide in-depth insights into the experiences, perspectives, and perceptions of key stakeholders affected by government policies. They help analysts understand the context, nuances, and complexities of policy implementation, as well as the lived experiences of individuals and communities."

As the lecture continued, Dr. Hayes guided his students through examples of policy analysis in practice, highlighting the strengths, limitations, and ethical considerations associated with different methodologies.

"As you explore the methodologies for policy analysis," Dr. Hayes concluded, "consider the importance of using a combination of quantitative and qualitative approaches to gain a comprehensive understanding of policy effectiveness and impact. By leveraging a diverse array of methods, we can produce more robust, nuanced, and actionable policy analysis findings."

The students left the lecture hall, their minds buzzing

with newfound insights into the methodologies used to assess government policies. Dr. Hayes watched them go, knowing that they had gained valuable tools for analyzing and improving public policies in the real world.

Cost-Benefit Analysis

Dr. Robert Hayes, a paragon of academic authority, delved into the intricacies of cost-benefit analysis, a cornerstone methodology in evaluating public policies. This subpoint illuminated the systematic process of weighing the costs and benefits of policy alternatives, essential for informing decision-making and resource allocation in modern governance.

"Good morning, class," Dr. Hayes greeted, his voice echoing with scholarly confidence. "Today, we dive into the world of cost-benefit analysis, a powerful tool for assessing the economic efficiency and societal impact of government policies."

He clicked to the first slide, revealing the title: "Cost-Benefit Analysis."

"Cost-benefit analysis," Dr. Hayes began, "is a systematic approach to evaluating the relative merits of policy alternatives by comparing their costs and benefits. It provides policymakers with valuable insights into the economic efficiency, social value, and distributional impacts of proposed policies, enabling them to make more informed decisions about resource allocation and policy design."

As he spoke, images of financial spreadsheets, economic models, and policy scenarios filled the screen, illustrating the analytical process of cost-benefit analysis.

"The first step in cost-benefit analysis is to identify and quantify all relevant costs and benefits associated with each policy alternative," Dr. Hayes continued. "Costs may include direct expenditures, opportunity costs, and externalities, while benefits may encompass increased productivity, improved health outcomes, and enhanced social welfare."

A hand shot up from a student named Emily. "How do analysts account for intangible costs and benefits in cost-benefit analysis?"

"Accounting for intangible costs and benefits can be challenging," Dr. Hayes acknowledged, "but analysts use various techniques such as contingent valuation, stated preference surveys, and shadow pricing to estimate the monetary value of intangible factors such as environmental quality, health improvements, and quality of life enhancements."

He clicked to the next slide, which read: "Calculating Net Present Value."

"The next step is to calculate the net present value (NPV) of each policy alternative," Dr. Hayes explained. "NPV is a measure of the total value generated by a policy after accounting for the time value of money. By discounting future costs and benefits to their present value using an appropriate discount rate, analysts can determine whether a policy is economically viable and socially desirable over the long term."

A student named Marcus raised his hand. "How do policy-makers use NPV to inform decision-making?"

"Policymakers use NPV as a decision criterion to compare the economic efficiency of different policy alternatives," Dr. Hayes replied. "Policies with positive NPV are considered economically viable and socially desirable, indicating that their benefits outweigh their costs. Policymakers may also consider other factors such as distributional equity, political feasibility, and legal constraints when making decisions about policy adoption and implementation."

He clicked to the next slide, which displayed the phrase: "Sensitivity Analysis."

"The final step is to conduct sensitivity analysis to assess the robustness of the results," Dr. Hayes said. "Sensitivity analysis involves varying key assumptions, parameters, and inputs to test the sensitivity of the results to changes in these factors. By identifying critical uncertainties and their potential impacts on the findings, analysts can provide policymakers with more reliable and nuanced insights into the implications of their policy decisions."

As the lecture continued, Dr. Hayes guided his students through examples of cost-benefit analysis in practice, high-lighting its applications, limitations, and ethical considera-tions.

"As you explore cost-benefit analysis," Dr. Hayes concluded, "consider the importance of transparency, rigor, and objectiv-ity in conducting and interpreting the analysis. By adhering to best practices and ethical standards, we can ensure that cost-benefit analysis serves as a valuable tool for informing decision-making and promoting the public good."

The students left the lecture hall, their minds enriched by the principles of cost-benefit analysis presented by Dr. Hayes. Dr. Hayes watched them go, knowing that they had gained valuable insights into the complexities of evaluating public policies and their impacts on society.

Program Evaluation Techniques

Dr. Robert Hayes, an eminent figure in the field of public policy analysis, delved into the realm of program evaluation techniques, essential for assessing the effectiveness, efficiency, and impact of government programs. This subpoint illuminated the diverse methodologies used to rigorously evaluate the outcomes and outcomes of public interventions, offering valuable insights into the complexities of program evaluation in modern governance.

"Good morning, class," Dr. Hayes greeted, his voice resonating with scholarly authority. "Today, we explore the methodologies used to evaluate the effectiveness and impact of government programs, essential for ensuring accountability, transparency, and continuous improvement in public service delivery."

He clicked to the first slide, unveiling the title: "Program Evaluation Techniques."

"Program evaluation," Dr. Hayes began, "is the systematic assessment of the design, implementation, and outcomes of government programs to determine their effectiveness, efficiency, and impact. It involves gathering and analyzing data, measuring performance against predetermined criteria, and making evidence-based recommendations for program improvement."

As he spoke, images of evaluation frameworks, impact assessments, and performance indicators filled the screen, illustrating the diverse array of techniques used in program evaluation.

"The first technique we'll explore is outcome evaluation," Dr. Hayes continued. "Outcome evaluation focuses on assessing the intended outcomes and impacts of a program, such as changes in knowledge, attitudes, behavior, or social conditions. It seeks to answer questions about whether the program achieved its intended goals and produced desired outcomes for participants and stakeholders."

A hand shot up from a student named Emily. "How do evaluators determine causality in outcome evaluation?"

"Determining causality in outcome evaluation can be challenging," Dr. Hayes acknowledged, "but evaluators use various methods such as randomized controlled trials, quasi-experimental designs, and matching techniques to establish causal relationships between program interventions and observed outcomes. By carefully controlling for confounding factors and biases, evaluators can provide more robust evidence of program effectiveness."

He clicked to the next slide, which read: "Process Evaluation."

"The next technique is process evaluation," Dr. Hayes explained. "Process evaluation focuses on assessing the implementation, fidelity, and quality of program activities and services. It seeks to answer questions about how well a program was implemented, whether it reached its intended target population, and whether it delivered services as intended."

A student named Marcus raised his hand. "How do evaluators measure program fidelity and quality?"

"Evaluators measure program fidelity and quality by collecting data on various implementation factors such as adherence to program protocols, dosage or intensity of services delivered, and participant engagement and satisfaction," Dr. Hayes replied. "They may use observation, interviews, surveys, and document reviews to assess the extent to which program activities were implemented as planned and whether they met established quality standards."

He clicked to the next slide, which displayed the phrase: "Cost-Effectiveness Analysis."

"The final technique we'll explore is cost-effectiveness analysis," Dr. Hayes said. "Cost-effectiveness analysis compares the costs and outcomes of program alternatives to determine their relative efficiency and value for money. It helps policymakers identify the most cost-effective interventions for achieving desired outcomes and allocate resources more efficiently."

As the lecture continued, Dr. Hayes guided his students through examples of program evaluation in practice, highlighting the strengths, limitations, and ethical considerations associated with different techniques.

"As you explore program evaluation techniques," Dr. Hayes concluded, "consider the importance of using a combination of methods to gain a comprehensive understanding of program effectiveness and impact. By leveraging diverse evaluation techniques, we can ensure that government programs are evidence-based, accountable, and responsive to the needs of society."

The students left the lecture hall, their minds buzzing with newfound insights into the methodologies used to evaluate government programs. Dr. Hayes watched them go, knowing that they had gained valuable tools for assessing the effectiveness and impact of public interventions in the real world.

Utilizing Evaluation Techniques for Policy Improvement

Dr. Robert Hayes, a respected figure in the realm of public policy analysis, delved into the crucial role of evaluation techniques in driving policy improvement. This subpoint illuminated how policymakers and practitioners can leverage evaluation findings to enhance the design, implementation, and outcomes of government programs, fostering continuous learning and innovation in modern governance.

"Good morning, class," Dr. Hayes greeted, his voice exuding scholarly wisdom. "Today, we explore how evaluation techniques can be utilized to drive policy improvement and enhance the effectiveness of government programs."

He clicked to the first slide, unveiling the title: "Utilizing Evaluation Techniques for Policy Improvement."

"Evaluation techniques," Dr. Hayes began, "provide policymakers and practitioners with valuable insights into the strengths, weaknesses, and unintended consequences of government programs. By systematically assessing program performance and outcomes, policymakers can identify areas for improvement, refine program design, and enhance service delivery to better meet the needs of citizens."

As he spoke, images of policymakers reviewing evaluation reports, stakeholders discussing findings, and program managers implementing recommendations filled the screen, illustrating the collaborative process of utilizing evaluation techniques for policy improvement.

"The first step in utilizing evaluation techniques for policy improvement is to disseminate evaluation findings to relevant stakeholders," Dr. Hayes continued. "By sharing evaluation reports, data, and insights with policymakers, program managers, and other stakeholders, evaluators can ensure that decision-makers are informed about program performance and are aware of opportunities for improvement."

A hand shot up from a student named Emily. "How can policymakers ensure that evaluation findings are acted upon and lead to meaningful changes in policy and practice?"

"Policymakers can ensure that evaluation findings lead to meaningful changes by fostering a culture of evidence-based decision-making and accountability," Dr. Hayes replied. "They can establish mechanisms for tracking and monitoring the implementation of evaluation recommendations, allocate resources for program improvements, and provide incentives for innovation and learning. By prioritizing responsiveness and adaptability, policymakers can use evaluation findings to drive continuous improvement and innovation in government programs."

He clicked to the next slide, which read: "Iterative Learning and Adaptation."

"The next step is to promote iterative learning and adaptation," Dr. Hayes explained. "Evaluation is an ongoing process that should be integrated into the policymaking cycle. By conducting regular evaluations, soliciting feedback from stakeholders, and adapting programs based on evaluation findings, policymakers can ensure that government programs remain responsive to changing needs and circumstances."

A student named Marcus raised his hand. "How can policymakers balance the need for innovation and experimentation with the imperative for accountability and risk management?"

"Policymakers can balance the need for innovation and accountability by adopting a balanced approach to program design and implementation," Dr. Hayes replied. "They can use techniques such as pilot testing, phased implementation, and randomized controlled trials to test new ideas and innovations in a controlled environment before scaling them up. By carefully managing risks and monitoring outcomes, policymakers can minimize the potential for unintended consequences while maximizing the benefits of innovation."

He clicked to the next slide, which displayed the phrase: "Building Evaluation Capacity."

"The final step is to build evaluation capacity within government agencies and organizations," Dr. Hayes said. "By investing in training, technical assistance, and resources for evaluation, policymakers can empower staff to conduct rigorous evaluations, analyze data effectively, and use evaluation findings to inform decision-making and improve program performance."

As the lecture continued, Dr. Hayes guided his students through examples of how evaluation techniques have been utilized to drive policy improvement in various government programs and initiatives, highlighting the importance of collaboration, transparency, and accountability in the process.

"As you explore the role of evaluation techniques in policy improvement," Dr. Hayes concluded, "consider the potential for evaluation to drive innovation, foster learning, and enhance the effectiveness of government programs. By leveraging evaluation findings to inform decision-making and practice, we can ensure that public policies and programs are responsive, accountable, and impactful."

The students left the lecture hall, inspired by the possibilities of using evaluation techniques to drive positive change in government. Dr. Hayes watched them go, knowing that they had gained valuable insights into the transformative potential of evaluation in modern governance.

Case Studies in Policy Evaluation

Dr. Robert Hayes, an esteemed authority in public policy analysis, embarked on a journey through compelling case studies in policy evaluation. This subpoint illuminated real-world examples of how evaluation techniques have been applied to assess the effectiveness, efficiency, and impact of government policies, offering valuable lessons and insights for practitioners and policymakers alike.

"Good morning, class," Dr. Hayes greeted, his voice echoing with scholarly enthusiasm. "Today, we delve into case studies in policy evaluation, exploring how evaluation techniques have been used to assess the outcomes and impacts of government policies in diverse contexts."

He clicked to the first slide, unveiling the title: "Case Studies in Policy Evaluation."

"Case studies," Dr. Hayes began, "provide rich insights into the complexities and challenges of evaluating government policies in practice. By examining real-world examples, we can gain a deeper understanding of the methods, approaches, and lessons learned from policy evaluation efforts."

As he spoke, images of policymakers, researchers, and stakeholders engaged in evaluation activities filled the screen, illustrating the diverse range of case studies to be explored.

"The first case study we'll examine is the evaluation of a youth employment program in a urban setting," Dr. Hayes continued. "This program aimed to provide job training and placement services to disadvantaged youth in the community, with the goal of improving employment outcomes and reducing poverty."

A hand shot up from a student named Emily. "How was the evaluation conducted, and what were the key findings?"

"The evaluation employed a mixed-methods approach, combining quantitative surveys with qualitative interviews and focus groups," Dr. Hayes replied. "Researchers assessed participants' employment outcomes, earnings, and educational attainment before and after participating in the program, as well as their perceptions of program effectiveness and impact. Key findings revealed that while the program successfully placed participants in jobs, long-term outcomes were mixed, highlighting the need for ongoing support and intervention to address systemic barriers to employment."

He clicked to the next slide, which read: "Impact Evaluation of a Health Policy."

"The next case study is an impact evaluation of a health policy aimed at reducing smoking rates among adolescents," Dr. Hayes explained. "This policy implemented a combination of education, taxation, and regulation measures to discourage youth smoking and promote public health."

A student named Marcus raised his hand. "What were the key findings of the impact evaluation, and how were they used to inform policy decisions?"

"The impact evaluation found that the policy was successful in reducing smoking rates among adolescents and improving public health outcomes," Dr. Hayes replied. "Researchers observed significant declines in youth smoking prevalence, tobacco consumption, and related health issues following the implementation of the policy. These findings were instrumental in demonstrating the effectiveness of the policy interventions and providing policymakers with evidence to support the continuation and expansion of similar initiatives in other jurisdictions."

He clicked to the next slide, which displayed the phrase: "Process Evaluation of a Social Welfare Program."

"The final case study is a process evaluation of a social welfare program aimed at providing financial assistance to low-income families," Dr. Hayes said. "This evaluation focused on assessing the implementation, delivery, and accessibility of program services, as well as the experiences and satisfaction of program participants."

As the lecture continued, Dr. Hayes guided his students through a series of case studies, each offering unique insights into the complexities and nuances of policy evaluation in practice. From youth employment programs to health policies and social welfare initiatives, these case studies provided valuable lessons and best practices for evaluating government policies and programs.

"As you explore these case studies," Dr. Hayes concluded, "consider the importance of using a combination of methods and approaches to gain a comprehensive understanding of policy effectiveness and impact. By learning from real-world examples, we can improve the rigor, relevance, and utility of policy evaluation efforts, ultimately leading to better-informed decision-making and improved outcomes for society."

The students left the lecture hall, their minds buzzing with newfound insights from the captivating case studies presented by Dr. Hayes. Dr. Hayes watched them go, knowing that they had gained valuable perspectives on the complexities of evaluating government policies and programs in the real world.

13

Chapter 13: Comparative Public Administration

Approaches to Comparative Public Administration

D r. Robert Hayes, a distinguished scholar in the field of public administration, embarked on an enlightening exploration of the diverse approaches to comparative public administration. This subpoint illuminated the theoretical frameworks and methodological approaches used to analyze and compare administrative systems across different countries and contexts, offering valuable insights into the complexities of governance in a globalized world.

"Good morning, class," Dr. Hayes greeted, his voice resonating with scholarly enthusiasm. "Today, we embark on a journey through the fascinating realm of comparative public administration, exploring the various approaches and perspectives used to study administrative systems around the world."

He clicked to the first slide, unveiling the title: "Approaches to Comparative Public Administration."

"Comparative public administration," Dr. Hayes began, "is the systematic study of administrative systems, structures, and practices across different countries and contexts. It seeks to identify common patterns, variations, and trends in governance, shedding light on the factors that shape administrative performance and outcomes."

As he spoke, images of government buildings, policy documents, and administrative processes from around the world filled the screen, illustrating the diverse range of administrative systems to be explored.

"The first approach we'll examine is the institutional approach," Dr. Hayes continued. "This approach focuses on analyzing the formal structures, processes, and functions of government institutions, such as executive agencies, legislatures, and judiciaries. It seeks to understand how institutional arrangements influence policy formulation, implementation, and enforcement in different political systems."

A hand shot up from a student named Emily. "How do scholars apply the institutional approach in comparative public administration?"

"Scholars apply the institutional approach by conducting detailed comparative analyses of government institutions across different countries," Dr. Hayes replied. "They examine factors such as the division of powers, separation of functions, and checks and balances within and between branches of government. By comparing institutional arrangements and their impact on administrative performance, scholars can identify best practices and lessons learned for improving governance and public service delivery."

He clicked to the next slide, which read: "Cultural Approach."

"The next approach is the cultural approach," Dr. Hayes explained. "This approach focuses on understanding the cultural values, norms, and traditions that shape administrative behavior and decision-making in different societies. It recognizes that cultural factors play a significant role in shaping administrative practices, attitudes, and relationships, influencing how governments interact with citizens and address public needs."

A student named Marcus raised his hand. "How do cultural differences impact administrative systems, and what are the implications for comparative analysis?"

"Cultural differences can impact administrative systems in various ways," Dr. Hayes replied. "They can influence attitudes toward authority, perceptions of accountability, and expectations of government responsiveness. For example, in societies with strong hierarchical traditions, administrative decision-making may be more centralized and top-down, whereas in societies with a strong emphasis on individualism and autonomy, administrative decision-making may be more decentralized and participatory. By recognizing and accounting for cultural differences, comparative public administration scholars can gain a deeper understanding of how administrative systems operate in diverse cultural contexts."

He clicked to the next slide, which displayed the phrase: "Institutional-Functional Approach."

"The final approach we'll explore is the institutional-functional approach," Dr. Hayes said. "This approach combines elements of the institutional and functional approaches, focusing on the interaction between formal institutions and their functional roles in achieving administrative goals. It seeks to understand how institutional arrangements contribute to administrative effectiveness, efficiency, and legitimacy, taking into account both structural and functional dimensions of governance."

As the lecture continued, Dr. Hayes guided his students through a series of case studies and examples, each highlighting the complexities and nuances of comparative public administration. From the analysis of government institutions to the examination of cultural influences and functional roles, these approaches offered valuable insights into the diversity of administrative systems and practices around the world.

"As you explore these approaches," Dr. Hayes concluded, "consider the importance of adopting a multidisciplinary and holistic perspective on comparative public administration. By integrating insights from political science, sociology, anthropology, and other disciplines, we can gain a richer understanding of the complexities of governance in a globalized world."

The students left the lecture hall, their minds buzzing with newfound insights from the captivating exploration of comparative public administration presented by Dr. Hayes. Dr. Hayes watched them go, knowing that they had gained valuable perspectives on the complexities of governance in diverse cultural and institutional contexts.

Administrative Systems Around the World

Dr. Robert Hayes, a renowned expert in public administration, embarked on a captivating exploration of administrative systems around the world. This subpoint delved into the diverse structures, functions, and practices of government bureaucracies across different countries and regions, offering valuable insights into the complexities of governance in an increasingly interconnected world.

"Good morning, class," Dr. Hayes greeted, his voice brimming with scholarly enthusiasm. "Today, we continue our journey through the fascinating realm of comparative public administration, focusing on the diverse administrative systems that exist around the world."

He clicked to the first slide, unveiling the title: "Administrative Systems Around the World."

"Administrative systems," Dr. Hayes began, "vary widely across different countries and regions, reflecting unique historical, cultural, and institutional contexts. From the centralized bureaucracies of authoritarian regimes to the decentralized networks of federal democracies, each administrative system has its own strengths, weaknesses, and peculiarities."

As he spoke, images of government buildings, civil servants, and administrative processes from various countries filled the screen, illustrating the diversity of administrative systems to be explored.

"The first type of administrative system we'll examine is the unitary system," Dr. Hayes continued. "In a unitary system, power and authority are concentrated at the national level, with subordinate units such as provinces, regions, or municipalities serving as administrative extensions of the central government. This centralized model of governance is common in countries with strong traditions of centralization and uniformity, such as France and Japan."

A hand shot up from a student named Emily. "How does the unitary system differ from federalism, and what are the implications for governance?"

"The unitary system differs from federalism in that it emphasizes centralization and uniformity, whereas federalism emphasizes decentralization and autonomy," Dr. Hayes replied. "In a unitary system, the central government exercises significant control over subnational units, making key decisions and setting policies that apply uniformly across the country. In contrast, federalism divides power and authority between the national government and subnational entities, allowing for greater autonomy and flexibility in policy-making and service delivery. The choice between unitary and federal systems has important implications for governance, with unitary systems often prized for their efficiency and consistency, while federal systems are valued for their responsiveness and adaptability to local needs."

He clicked to the next slide, which read: "Decentralized Systems."

"The next type of administrative system is the decentralized system," Dr. Hayes explained. "In a decentralized system, power and authority are dispersed among multiple levels of government, with subnational entities such as states, provinces, or municipalities enjoying significant autonomy and decision-making authority. This model of governance is common in federal countries such as the United States, Germany, and Canada, where subnational governments play a key role in policy-making and service delivery."

A student named Marcus raised his hand. "What are the advantages and disadvantages of decentralized systems, and how do they compare to unitary systems?"

"Decentralized systems offer advantages such as greater responsiveness to local needs, increased citizen participation, and opportunities for innovation and experimentation," Dr. Hayes replied. "However, they also pose challenges such as coordination problems, administrative complexity, and potential for duplication and overlap. Compared to unitary systems, decentralized systems tend to be more flexible and adaptable to diverse local contexts, but they may also experience challenges in coordinating policy and service delivery across multiple levels of government."

He clicked to the next slide, which displayed the phrase: "Hybrid Systems."

"The final type of administrative system we'll explore is the hybrid system," Dr. Hayes said. "Hybrid systems combine elements of both unitary and federal models, blending centralized and decentralized features to suit the unique needs and circumstances of particular countries or regions. These systems often reflect historical legacies, cultural traditions, and political compromises, offering a middle ground between the extremes of centralization and decentralization."

As the lecture continued, Dr. Hayes guided his students through a series of case studies and examples, each highlighting the unique characteristics and challenges of administrative systems around the world. From unitary and federal models to decentralized and hybrid arrangements, these systems offered valuable insights into the complexities of governance in diverse political and institutional contexts.

"As you explore these administrative systems," Dr. Hayes concluded, "consider the implications for governance, policy-making, and service delivery in different countries and regions. By understanding the strengths and weaknesses of various administrative models, we can gain a deeper appreciation for the complexities of governance in an interconnected world."

The students left the lecture hall, their minds buzzing with newfound insights from the captivating exploration of administrative systems presented by Dr. Hayes. Dr. Hayes watched them go, knowing that they had gained valuable perspectives on the diversity and complexity of governance around the world.

Best Practices and Lessons Learned

Dr. Robert Hayes, an esteemed scholar in public administration, led his students on a journey through the realm of best practices and lessons learned in comparative public administration. This subpoint illuminated the valuable insights gleaned from the study of administrative systems around the world, offering guidance for policymakers and practitioners seeking to improve governance and public service delivery.

"Good morning, class," Dr. Hayes greeted, his voice resonating with scholarly vigor. "Today, we continue our exploration of comparative public administration by examining best practices and lessons learned from the study of administrative systems around the world."

He clicked to the first slide, revealing the title: "Best Practices and Lessons Learned."

"As we've discussed," Dr. Hayes began, "comparative public

administration offers valuable insights into the diverse structures, functions, and practices of government bureaucracies across different countries and regions. By analyzing the successes and failures of administrative systems around the world, we can identify best practices and lessons learned that inform our understanding of effective governance and public service delivery."

As he spoke, images of government officials, policy reports, and administrative reforms filled the screen, illustrating the wealth of knowledge to be explored.

"The first lesson we've learned," Dr. Hayes continued, "is the importance of transparency and accountability in governance. Transparent and accountable institutions are essential for building public trust, promoting integrity, and ensuring effective oversight of government actions. Countries that have implemented robust mechanisms for transparency and accountability, such as open data initiatives, whistleblower protections, and independent oversight bodies, have seen improvements in governance and public service delivery."

A hand shot up from a student named Emily. "How do countries promote transparency and accountability, and what are the challenges they face?"

"Promoting transparency and accountability requires a multifaceted approach," Dr. Hayes replied. "Countries often enact legislation to ensure access to information and establish oversight mechanisms to monitor government actions. However, challenges such as corruption, lack of political will, and resource constraints can impede efforts to promote transparency and accountability. Overcoming these challenges requires sustained commitment from policymakers, civil society, and international partners."

He clicked to the next slide, which read: "Innovation and Adaptation."

"The next lesson we've learned is the importance of innovation and adaptation in governance," Dr. Hayes explained. "Administrative systems that embrace innovation and adapt to changing circumstances are better equipped to address complex challenges and deliver quality services to citizens. Countries that have invested in digital technologies, streamlined bureaucratic processes, and encouraged experimentation and learning have seen improvements in administrative performance and responsiveness."

A student named Marcus raised his hand. "How do countries foster innovation and adaptation in their administrative systems?"

"Countries foster innovation and adaptation through a combination of policies, practices, and cultural norms," Dr. Hayes replied. "They invest in research and development, encourage collaboration and knowledge sharing among government agencies, and create incentives for experimentation and risk-taking. Additionally, they promote a culture of learning and continuous improvement, where failures are viewed as opportunities for growth and innovation."

He clicked to the next slide, which displayed the phrase: "Collaboration and Partnership."

"The final lesson we'll explore is the importance of collaboration and partnership in governance," Dr. Hayes said. "Collaborative approaches involving government agencies, civil society organizations, the private sector, and international partners are essential for addressing complex challenges that transcend national borders. Countries that have embraced collaborative governance models, such as public-private partnerships, intergovernmental cooperation, and multilateral initiatives, have seen improvements in policy outcomes and service delivery."

As the lecture continued, Dr. Hayes guided his students through a series of case studies and examples, each highlighting best practices and lessons learned from the study of administrative systems around the world. From transparency and accountability to innovation and collaboration, these lessons offered valuable insights into the keys to effective governance in an interconnected world.

"As you reflect on these lessons," Dr. Hayes concluded, "consider how they can inform efforts to improve governance and public service delivery in your own communities and countries. By learning from the successes and failures of administrative systems around the world, we can build more transparent, innovative, and collaborative governance structures that better serve the needs of citizens."

The students left the lecture hall, their minds buzzing with newfound insights from the captivating exploration of best practices and lessons learned in comparative public administration presented by Dr. Hayes. Dr. Hayes watched them go, knowing that they had gained valuable perspectives on the keys to effective governance in an increasingly complex and interconnected world.

Impact of Cultural Differences on Administration

Dr. Robert Hayes, a distinguished scholar in public administration, delved into the intricate relationship between cultural differences and administrative practices. This subpoint explored how cultural norms, values, and traditions shape administrative behavior and decision-making in diverse societies, offering valuable insights into the complexities of governance in a multicultural world.

"Good morning, class," Dr. Hayes greeted, his voice infused with scholarly fervor. "Today, we continue our exploration of comparative public administration by examining the impact of cultural differences on administrative practices."

He clicked to the first slide, revealing the title: "Impact of Cultural Differences on Administration."

"Cultural differences," Dr. Hayes began, "play a significant role in shaping administrative systems and practices around the world. From attitudes toward authority and hierarchy to perceptions of accountability and transparency, cultural norms and values influence how governments operate and interact with citizens."

As he spoke, images of cultural ceremonies, traditional attire, and social gatherings from various countries filled the screen, illustrating the diversity of cultural influences to be explored.

"The first aspect of culture we'll examine is the concept of power distance," Dr. Hayes continued. "Power distance refers to the degree to which individuals in a society accept and expect unequal distributions of power and authority. In cultures with high power distance, such as many Asian and Middle Eastern societies, hierarchical relationships and deference to authority are valued, leading to centralized decision-making and top-down leadership styles in administrative practices."

A hand shot up from a student named Emily. "How does power distance affect administrative practices, and what are the implications for governance?"

"Power distance affects administrative practices in various

ways," Dr. Hayes replied. "In cultures with high power distance, administrative decision-making may be centralized, with little input from subordinates or stakeholders. This can lead to challenges in communication, collaboration, and innovation, as lower-ranking employees may be reluctant to challenge authority or offer dissenting opinions. Conversely, in cultures with low power distance, such as many Western societies, administrative decision-making may be more decentralized and participatory, allowing for greater input from diverse stakeholders and fostering a culture of transparency and accountability."

He clicked to the next slide, which read: "Individualism vs. Collectivism."

"The next cultural dimension we'll explore is individualism versus collectivism," Dr. Hayes explained. "Individualist cultures prioritize individual rights, autonomy, and self-expression, whereas collectivist cultures emphasize group harmony, cooperation, and social cohesion. These cultural differences can influence administrative practices in areas such as decision-making, conflict resolution, and communication."

A student named Marcus raised his hand. "How do individualist and collectivist cultures approach administrative decision-making differently?"

"In individualist cultures, administrative decision-making tends to be more decentralized and participatory, with individuals given autonomy and authority to make decisions based on their expertise and judgment," Dr. Hayes replied. "In collectivist cultures, decision-making may be more consensus-driven, with a focus on group harmony and consensus-building. This can lead to slower decision-making processes but may also foster greater buy-in and support from stakeholders."

He clicked to the next slide, which displayed the phrase: "Uncertainty Avoidance."

"The final cultural dimension we'll examine is uncertainty avoidance," Dr. Hayes said. "Uncertainty avoidance refers to the extent to which individuals in a society feel uncomfortable with ambiguity, unpredictability, and risk. Cultures with high uncertainty avoidance tend to have strict rules, procedures, and protocols to minimize uncertainty and maintain order, whereas cultures with low uncertainty avoidance are more tolerant of ambiguity and risk."

As the lecture continued, Dr. Hayes guided his students through a series of case studies and examples, each highlighting the impact of cultural differences on administrative practices in diverse societies. From power distance and individualism to uncertainty avoidance, these cultural dimensions offered valuable insights into the complexities of governance in a multicultural world.

"As you reflect on these cultural differences," Dr. Hayes concluded, "consider how they shape administrative practices and interactions in your own communities and countries. By understanding and appreciating cultural diversity, we can build more inclusive and effective administrative systems that better serve the needs of citizens from diverse backgrounds."

The students left the lecture hall, their minds buzzing with newfound insights from the captivating exploration of cultural differences in administrative practices presented by Dr. Hayes. Dr. Hayes watched them go, knowing that they had gained valuable perspectives on the complexities of governance in a multicultural world.

Global Trends in Public Administration

Dr. Robert Hayes, an eminent scholar in public administration, embarked on a captivating exploration of global trends shaping administrative practices around the world. This subpoint illuminated the evolving landscape of governance in the 21st century, offering valuable insights into the challenges and opportunities facing public administrators in an increasingly interconnected world.

"Good morning, class," Dr. Hayes greeted, his voice resonating with scholarly passion. "Today, we continue our journey through comparative public administration by examining global trends shaping administrative practices."

He clicked to the first slide, unveiling the title: "Global Trends in Public Administration."

"Public administration," Dr. Hayes began, "is constantly evolving in response to changes in technology, demographics, economics, and politics. From the rise of digital governance to the growing emphasis on sustainability and equity, global trends are reshaping the way governments operate and deliver services to citizens."

As he spoke, images of smart cities, sustainable development projects, and international conferences filled the screen, illustrating the breadth of global trends to be explored.

"The first trend we'll explore is the rise of digital governance," Dr. Hayes continued. "Digital technologies such as artificial intelligence, big data analytics, and blockchain are transforming administrative practices, enabling governments to deliver services more efficiently, engage citizens more effectively, and make data-driven decisions."

A hand shot up from a student named Emily. "How is digital

governance transforming administrative practices, and what are the implications for public administrators?"

"Digital governance is transforming administrative practices in various ways," Dr. Hayes replied. "For example, governments are using data analytics to identify trends and patterns, inform policy decisions, and improve service delivery. They're also leveraging digital platforms to engage citizens in decision-making processes, solicit feedback, and enhance transparency and accountability. However, digital governance also poses challenges such as data privacy concerns, digital divides, and cybersecurity risks, which public administrators must navigate effectively."

He clicked to the next slide, which read: "Sustainability and Environmental Governance."

"The next trend we'll examine is the growing emphasis on sustainability and environmental governance," Dr. Hayes explained. "As concerns about climate change, pollution, and natural resource depletion mount, governments are increasingly prioritizing sustainable development goals and integrating environmental considerations into administrative practices."

A student named Marcus raised his hand. "How are governments addressing sustainability and environmental governance, and what are the challenges they face?"

"Governments are addressing sustainability and environmental governance through a combination of policy initiatives, regulatory frameworks, and collaborative efforts with stakeholders," Dr. Hayes replied. "They're implementing measures such as renewable energy incentives, carbon pricing schemes, and sustainable urban planning practices to mitigate environmental impacts and promote resilience. However, challenges such as competing interests, resource constraints, and global coordination gaps pose obstacles to effective environmental governance."

He clicked to the next slide, which displayed the phrase: "Equity and Social Justice."

"The final trend we'll explore is the growing emphasis on equity and social justice," Dr. Hayes said. "As disparities in income, education, and access to services persist, governments are increasingly focused on addressing social inequities and advancing inclusive development agendas."

As the lecture continued, Dr. Hayes guided his students through a series of case studies and examples, each highlighting global trends shaping administrative practices and their implications for public administrators. From digital governance and sustainability to equity and social justice, these trends offered valuable insights into the challenges and opportunities facing governance in an interconnected world.

"As you reflect on these global trends," Dr. Hayes concluded, "consider how they are reshaping administrative practices and presenting new opportunities and challenges for public administrators. By staying informed and adaptive to these trends, we can better navigate the complexities of governance in a rapidly changing world."

The students left the lecture hall, their minds buzzing with newfound insights from the captivating exploration of global trends in public administration presented by Dr. Hayes. Dr. Hayes watched them go, knowing that they had gained valuable perspectives on the evolving landscape of governance in the 21st century.

Case Studies in International Public Administration

Dr. Robert Hayes, an esteemed scholar in public administration, guided his students through a series of compelling case studies in international public administration. This subpoint offered valuable insights into the diverse administrative challenges and innovative solutions implemented by governments around the world, showcasing the richness and complexity of global governance practices.

"Good morning, class," Dr. Hayes greeted, his voice brimming with scholarly enthusiasm. "Today, we conclude our exploration of comparative public administration with a series of case studies from around the world."

He clicked to the first slide, unveiling the title: "Case Studies in International Public Administration."

"Case studies," Dr. Hayes began, "provide us with real-world examples of administrative challenges, strategies, and outcomes, offering valuable lessons for policymakers and practitioners alike. From administrative reforms in Singapore to participatory budgeting in Brazil, these case studies showcase the diversity of approaches to governance and public service delivery."

As he spoke, images of government officials, community projects, and policy documents from various countries filled the screen, illustrating the breadth and depth of international public administration practices.

"The first case study we'll examine is administrative reform in Singapore," Dr. Hayes continued. "Singapore is renowned for its efficient and responsive bureaucracy, which has played a crucial role in the country's economic development and social progress. Through initiatives such as the Civil Service College and the Public Service Division, Singapore has invested in talent development, leadership training, and organizational excellence to build a world-class public service."

A hand shot up from a student named Emily. "What lessons can other countries learn from Singapore's administrative reforms?"

"Singapore's administrative reforms offer several valuable lessons for other countries," Dr. Hayes replied. "Firstly, investing in human capital and organizational capacity is essential for building a competent and responsive public service. Secondly, fostering a culture of innovation, excellence, and integrity is crucial for driving administrative performance and delivering quality services to citizens. Lastly, maintaining a strong political will and leadership commitment to administrative reform is essential for overcoming resistance to change and sustaining momentum for improvement."

He clicked to the next slide, which read: "Participatory Budgeting in Porto Alegre, Brazil."

"The next case study we'll explore is participatory budgeting in Porto Alegre, Brazil," Dr. Hayes explained. "Porto Alegre pioneered the practice of participatory budgeting, which allows citizens to directly participate in the allocation of public funds and decision-making processes. Through neighborhood assemblies, citizen councils, and public consultations, Porto Alegre has empowered residents to shape budget priorities, address community needs, and enhance transparency and accountability in government spending."

A student named Marcus raised his hand. "How has participatory budgeting impacted governance and public service delivery in Porto Alegre?"

"Participatory budgeting has had a significant impact on governance and public service delivery in Porto Alegre," Dr. Hayes replied. "By involving citizens in decision-making processes, the city has increased trust, legitimacy, and social cohesion, leading to greater citizen satisfaction and improved outcomes in service delivery. Additionally, participatory budgeting has helped prioritize investments in underserved communities, address inequality, and promote inclusive development agendas."

He clicked to the next slide, which displayed the phrase: "E-Government in Estonia."

"The final case study we'll examine is e-government in Estonia," Dr. Hayes said. "Estonia is a global leader in digital governance, with innovative initiatives such as e-residency, digital signatures, and online voting. Through investments in digital infrastructure, cybersecurity, and e-services, Estonia has transformed administrative processes, improved efficiency, and enhanced citizen engagement and satisfaction."

As the lecture continued, Dr. Hayes guided his students through a series of case studies and examples, each highlighting the diverse administrative challenges and innovative solutions implemented by governments around the world. From administrative reform in Singapore to participatory budgeting in Brazil and e-government in Estonia, these case studies offered valuable insights into the richness and complexity of global governance practices.

"As you reflect on these case studies," Dr. Hayes concluded, "consider how they can inform efforts to improve governance and public service delivery in your own communities and countries. By learning from the successes and failures of international public administration practices, we can build more effective, inclusive, and responsive governance structures that better serve the needs of citizens."

The students left the lecture hall, their minds buzzing with newfound insights from the captivating exploration of case studies in international public administration presented by Dr. Hayes. Dr. Hayes watched them go, knowing that they had gained valuable perspectives on the diverse approaches to governance and public service delivery implemented by governments around the world.

14

Chapter 14: Public Administration in Crisis Management

Types of Public Crises

Dr. Emily Carter, a seasoned expert in crisis management, delved into the intricate landscape of public crises and their management. This subpoint illuminated the diverse nature of crises faced by governments worldwide, offering valuable insights into the strategies and challenges of crisis response and recovery.

"Good afternoon, everyone," Dr. Carter greeted, her voice carrying a sense of urgency tempered with expertise. "Today, we embark on a journey through the tumultuous terrain of crisis management, beginning with an exploration of the various types of public crises."

She clicked to the first slide, unveiling the title: "Types of Public Crises."

"Crises," Dr. Carter began, "come in many forms, each presenting unique challenges and requiring tailored responses from public administrators. From natural disasters to pandemics and political unrest, governments must be prepared to navigate a diverse array of crises to safeguard the well-being of their citizens and maintain social order."

As she spoke, images of hurricanes, protests, and health emergencies flashed across the screen, illustrating the breadth and complexity of public crises to be explored.

"The first type of public crisis we'll examine is natural disasters," Dr. Carter continued. "Natural disasters such as hurricanes, earthquakes, floods, and wildfires pose significant threats to public safety, infrastructure, and economic stability. Governments must develop robust preparedness and response plans to mitigate the impact of these disasters and ensure timely and effective assistance to affected communities."

A hand shot up from a student named Marcus. "How do governments prepare for and respond to natural disasters, and what are the key challenges they face?"

"Governments prepare for natural disasters through a combination of risk assessment, planning, and coordination with emergency response agencies and stakeholders," Dr. Carter replied. "Preparedness measures may include building resilient infrastructure, conducting evacuation drills, stockpiling emergency supplies, and educating the public about disaster risks and preparedness strategies. However, challenges such as limited resources, coordination gaps, and uncertainty about the scale and timing of disasters can complicate response efforts and exacerbate the impact on affected communities."

She clicked to the next slide, which read: "Public Health Emergencies."

"The next type of public crisis we'll explore is public health emergencies," Dr. Carter explained. "Public health emergencies such as pandemics, disease outbreaks, and bioterrorism threats can have devastating consequences for public health, healthcare systems, and socio-economic stability. Governments must implement proactive measures to prevent, detect, and respond to public health threats, including surveillance, vaccination campaigns, and capacity-building in healthcare infrastructure and personnel."

A student named Emily raised her hand. "How do governments coordinate response efforts during public health emergencies, and what are the key considerations in managing these crises?"

"During public health emergencies, governments coordinate response efforts through multi-agency task forces, intergovernmental cooperation, and partnerships with international organizations and public health authorities," Dr. Carter replied. "Key considerations in managing these crises include early detection and containment of the outbreak, effective communication with the public about risks and preventive measures, equitable access to healthcare services and resources, and maintaining essential services and supply chains to support response efforts."

She clicked to the next slide, which displayed the phrase: "Political Unrest and Civil Unrest."

"The final type of public crisis we'll examine is political unrest and civil unrest," Dr. Carter said. "Political unrest such as protests, riots, and civil disobedience can pose significant challenges to governance and public order, threatening stability, and security. Governments must balance the rights of citizens to peaceful assembly and expression with the need to maintain law and order, protect public safety, and uphold democratic principles."

As the lecture continued, Dr. Carter guided her students through a series of case studies and examples, each highlighting the diverse nature of public crises and the strategies employed by governments to manage and mitigate their impact. From natural disasters and public health emergencies to political unrest and civil unrest, these crises offered valuable insights into the complexities of crisis management and the importance of preparedness, coordination, and resilience in safeguarding the well-being of communities and nations.

"As you reflect on these types of public crises," Dr. Carter concluded, "consider the challenges and opportunities they present for governments and public administrators. By understanding the nature of crises and developing effective response plans and strategies, we can better protect lives, preserve livelihoods, and build more resilient and adaptive societies."

The students left the lecture hall, their minds buzzing with newfound insights from the captivating exploration of types of public crises presented by Dr. Carter. Dr. Carter watched them go, knowing that they had gained valuable perspectives on the challenges and complexities of crisis management in an increasingly uncertain world.

Crisis Management Frameworks

Dr. Emily Carter, a seasoned expert in crisis management, continued her exploration of crisis management by delving into the frameworks that guide governments in navigating crises. This subpoint illuminated the structured approaches and strategies employed by public administrators to effectively respond to and recover from crises, ensuring the resilience and stability of communities and nations.

"Welcome back, everyone," Dr. Carter greeted, her tone poised and authoritative. "In our journey through crisis management, we now turn our attention to the frameworks that provide a structured approach to managing crises."

She clicked to the first slide, unveiling the title: "Crisis Management Frameworks."

"Crisis management," Dr. Carter began, "requires a systematic and coordinated approach to identify, assess, respond to, and recover from crises. Various frameworks provide guidance to governments and organizations in managing crises effectively, ensuring timely and coordinated action to protect lives, property, and critical infrastructure."

As she spoke, diagrams outlining crisis management frameworks and images of emergency response teams in action appeared on the screen, illustrating the structured approaches to crisis management to be explored.

"The first framework we'll examine is the Incident Command System (ICS)," Dr. Carter continued. "The ICS is a standardized approach used by emergency response agencies to manage incidents, regardless of their size or complexity. It establishes clear command structures, communication protocols, and operational procedures to facilitate coordinated response efforts and ensure effective resource allocation and deployment."

A hand shot up from a student named Marcus. "How does the Incident Command System operate during crises, and what are its key components?"

"The Incident Command System operates by establishing a unified command structure, with designated roles and responsibilities for incident commanders, operations chiefs, planning sections, logistics coordinators, and other key personnel," Dr. Carter replied. "Key components of the ICS include the Incident Action Plan (IAP), which outlines objectives, strategies, and tactics for managing the incident; the Incident Communications Plan, which establishes communication protocols and channels; and the Incident Management Team, which coordinates response activities and allocates resources based on operational priorities."

She clicked to the next slide, which read: "Comprehensive Emergency Management."

"The next framework we'll explore is Comprehensive Emergency Management," Dr. Carter explained. "Comprehensive Emergency Management is a holistic approach to crisis management that encompasses four phases: mitigation, preparedness, response, and recovery. It emphasizes proactive measures to reduce risks, enhance resilience, and build capacity to respond to and recover from crises effectively."

A student named Emily raised her hand. "How does Comprehensive Emergency Management address the different phases of crisis management, and what are the key strategies in each phase?"

"Comprehensive Emergency Management addresses the different phases of crisis management through a combination of proactive and reactive measures," Dr. Carter replied. "During the mitigation phase, governments identify and assess risks, implement measures to reduce vulnerabilities, and build community resilience through education, training, and infrastructure improvements. In the preparedness phase, they develop emergency response plans, conduct drills and exercises, and build partnerships with stakeholders to enhance coordination and communication. In the response phase, they activate emergency operations centers, mobilize resources, and implement response plans to address immediate threats and protect lives and property. Finally, in the recovery phase, they assess damages, restore essential services, support affected communities, and implement measures to enhance long-term resilience and preparedness for future crises."

She clicked to the next slide, which displayed the phrase: "National Response Framework."

"The final framework we'll examine is the National Response Framework," Dr. Carter said. "The National Response Framework is a comprehensive guide for how the nation responds to all types of disasters and emergencies. It outlines the roles and responsibilities of federal, state, local, tribal, and territorial governments, as well as private sector and non-governmental organizations, in coordinating response efforts and supporting affected communities."

As the lecture continued, Dr. Carter guided her students through a detailed exploration of crisis management frameworks, highlighting their key components, principles, and applications in real-world scenarios. From the Incident Command System to Comprehensive Emergency Management and the National Response Framework, these frameworks offered valuable insights into the structured approaches and strategies employed by governments to effectively manage crises and safeguard the well-being of communities and nations.

"As you reflect on these crisis management frameworks," Dr. Carter concluded, "consider their utility in guiding response efforts and enhancing resilience in the face of diverse and evolving threats. By adopting a systematic and coordinated approach to crisis management, we can better protect lives, preserve livelihoods, and build more resilient and adaptive societies."

The students left the lecture hall, their minds buzzing with newfound insights from the captivating exploration of crisis management frameworks presented by Dr. Carter. Dr. Carter watched them go, knowing that they had gained valuable perspectives on the structured approaches to crisis management that underpin effective response and recovery efforts in an increasingly uncertain world.

Role of Public Administrators in Crises

Dr. Emily Carter, an esteemed scholar in crisis management, delved into the pivotal role of public administrators in navigating crises. This subpoint illuminated the leadership, coordination, and decision-making responsibilities of public administrators in orchestrating effective crisis response and recovery efforts, ensuring the safety and well-being of communities and nations.

"Welcome back, everyone," Dr. Carter greeted, her voice emanating a sense of urgency and resolve. "As we continue our exploration of crisis management, we now turn our attention to the critical role of public administrators in addressing crises."

She clicked to the first slide, unveiling the title: "Role of Public Administrators in Crises."

"Public administrators," Dr. Carter began, "play a central role in managing crises, serving as the backbone of government response and recovery efforts. They are responsible for coordinating multi-agency response efforts, mobilizing resources, and making critical decisions to protect lives, property, and critical infrastructure during crises."

As she spoke, images of public administrators coordinating response efforts, providing assistance to affected communities, and making decisions in high-pressure situations filled the screen, illustrating the pivotal role of public administrators in crisis management.

"The first aspect of the role of public administrators in crises is leadership," Dr. Carter continued. "During crises, public administrators must provide clear and decisive leadership to guide response efforts, inspire confidence, and rally stakeholders behind a common purpose. They must communicate effectively with the public, stakeholders, and emergency response teams, providing timely and accurate information to inform decision-making and reassure the community."

A hand shot up from a student named Marcus. "How do public administrators exercise leadership during crises, and what are the key qualities of effective crisis leaders?"

"Public administrators exercise leadership during crises by demonstrating calmness under pressure, decisiveness in decision-making, and empathy for those affected by the crisis," Dr. Carter replied. "Key qualities of effective crisis leaders include strong communication skills, strategic thinking, adaptability, and the ability to build and maintain trust and collaboration among diverse stakeholders. They must also prioritize the safety and well-being of the public, even in the face of uncertainty and adversity."

She clicked to the next slide, which read: "Coordination and Collaboration."

"The next aspect of the role of public administrators in

crises is coordination and collaboration," Dr. Carter explained. "During crises, public administrators must coordinate response efforts across multiple agencies, jurisdictions, and sectors to ensure a unified and effective response. They must establish clear command structures, communication protocols, and operational procedures to facilitate collaboration and coordination among diverse stakeholders."

A student named Emily raised her hand. "How do public administrators coordinate response efforts during crises, and what are the key challenges they face?"

"Public administrators coordinate response efforts during crises through established emergency management systems, such as the Incident Command System or Emergency Operations Centers," Dr. Carter replied. "They establish multi-agency task forces, hold regular briefings and meetings, and utilize technology and information-sharing platforms to facilitate communication and coordination. However, challenges such as resource constraints, jurisdictional boundaries, and competing priorities can complicate coordination efforts and hinder the effectiveness of response operations."

She clicked to the next slide, which displayed the phrase: "Decision Making and Crisis Communication."

"The final aspect of the role of public administrators in crises is decision-making and crisis communication," Dr. Carter said. "During crises, public administrators must make timely and well-informed decisions to protect lives and mitigate the impact of the crisis. They must gather and analyze relevant information, assess risks, and consult with experts and stakeholders to inform decision-making. Additionally, they must communicate effectively with the public, providing clear guidance, updates, and reassurance to foster trust and cooperation."

As the lecture continued, Dr. Carter guided her students through a detailed exploration of the role of public administrators in crises, highlighting the leadership, coordination, and decision-making responsibilities that underpin effective crisis response and recovery efforts. From providing clear and decisive leadership to coordinating multi-agency response efforts and making critical decisions under pressure, public administrators play a pivotal role in safeguarding the well-being of communities and nations in times of crisis.

"As you reflect on the role of public administrators in crises," Dr. Carter concluded, "consider the challenges and opportunities they face in orchestrating effective response and recovery efforts. By embracing their leadership responsibilities, fostering collaboration among stakeholders, and making well-informed decisions, public administrators can navigate crises with resilience and resolve, ensuring the safety and well-being of our communities and nations."

The students left the lecture hall, their minds buzzing with newfound insights from the captivating exploration of the role of public administrators in crises presented by Dr. Carter. Dr. Carter watched them go, knowing that they had gained valuable perspectives on the critical role of public administrators in guiding response and recovery efforts in an increasingly uncertain world.

Communication Strategies during Crises

Dr. Emily Carter, an expert in crisis management, delved into the crucial role of communication strategies during crises. This subpoint illuminated the importance of clear, timely, and transparent communication in providing vital information, managing public perceptions, and fostering trust and cooperation during times of crisis.

"Good afternoon, everyone," Dr. Carter greeted, her tone composed yet authoritative. "Today, we explore the critical role of communication strategies in crisis management."

She clicked to the first slide, revealing the title: "Communication Strategies during Crises."

"Effective communication is paramount during crises," Dr. Carter began. "It serves as a lifeline, providing vital information, calming fears, and guiding actions. Public administrators must employ strategic communication strategies to inform, reassure, and mobilize the public, stakeholders, and emergency response teams."

As she spoke, images of press conferences, emergency broadcasts, and social media updates flashed across the screen, illustrating the diverse communication channels and strategies used during crises.

"The first aspect of communication strategies during crises is clarity and transparency," Dr. Carter continued. "Public administrators must communicate clearly and transparently, providing accurate and up-to-date information about the crisis, its impact, and response efforts. They must address rumors and misinformation promptly, dispelling myths and ensuring that the public has access to reliable information to make informed decisions."

A hand shot up from a student named Marcus. "How do public administrators ensure clarity and transparency in their communication during crises, especially when information is constantly evolving?"

"Public administrators ensure clarity and transparency in

their communication by establishing communication protocols, designating spokespersons, and providing regular updates to the public," Dr. Carter replied. "They must acknowledge uncertainties and limitations in information, while emphasizing the steps being taken to address the crisis and protect public safety. Additionally, they must utilize multiple communication channels, such as press briefings, social media, websites, and emergency alerts, to reach diverse audiences and ensure that information is accessible and widely disseminated."

She clicked to the next slide, which read: "Timeliness and Consistency."

"The next aspect of communication strategies during crises is timeliness and consistency," Dr. Carter explained. "Public administrators must communicate in a timely manner, providing updates and guidance as soon as information becomes available. They must also ensure consistency in messaging across different communication channels and spokespersons, avoiding contradictory information that can undermine public trust and confidence."

A student named Emily raised her hand. "How do public administrators maintain consistency in their communication during crises, especially when there are multiple agencies and stakeholders involved?"

"Public administrators maintain consistency in their communication by establishing clear communication protocols and coordination mechanisms," Dr. Carter replied. "They must coordinate messaging and updates with other agencies and stakeholders to ensure alignment and consistency across response efforts. Additionally, they may utilize joint press conferences, interagency briefings, and communication platforms to convey unified messages and foster collaboration among diverse stakeholders."

She clicked to the next slide, which displayed the phrase: "Engagement and Empathy."

"The final aspect of communication strategies during crises is engagement and empathy," Dr. Carter said. "Public administrators must engage with the public and stakeholders, listening to their concerns, addressing their needs, and soliciting feedback to inform response efforts. They must demonstrate empathy and understanding for those affected by the crisis, acknowledging the challenges they face and providing support and assistance to alleviate their suffering."

As the lecture continued, Dr. Carter guided her students through a detailed exploration of communication strategies during crises, highlighting the importance of clarity, transparency, timeliness, consistency, engagement, and empathy in building trust and cooperation among stakeholders and fostering resilience in communities. From press briefings and emergency alerts to social media updates and community outreach initiatives, these communication strategies offered valuable insights into the vital role of communication in crisis management.

"As you reflect on these communication strategies," Dr. Carter concluded, "consider their impact on public perceptions, trust, and cooperation during crises. By employing clear, timely, and transparent communication strategies, public administrators can navigate crises with resilience and resolve, ensuring the safety and well-being of our communities and nations."

The students left the lecture hall, their minds buzzing with newfound insights from the captivating exploration of communication strategies during crises presented by Dr. Carter. Dr. Carter watched them go, knowing that they had gained valuable perspectives on the critical role of communication in guiding response and recovery efforts in an increasingly uncertain world.

Post-Crisis Recovery and Resilience

Dr. Emily Carter, a leading authority in crisis management, embarked on the exploration of post-crisis recovery and resilience. This subpoint illuminated the strategies and initiatives employed by public administrators to facilitate recovery, rebuild communities, and enhance resilience in the aftermath of crises, ensuring long-term sustainability and preparedness for future challenges.

"Welcome back, everyone," Dr. Carter greeted, her voice infused with determination and hope. "As we delve deeper into crisis management, we now shift our focus to post-crisis recovery and resilience."

She clicked to the first slide, unveiling the title: "Post-Crisis Recovery and Resilience."

"Recovery from crises is a complex and multifaceted process," Dr. Carter began. "It involves rebuilding communities, restoring essential services, and addressing the physical, emotional, and economic impacts of the crisis. Public administrators play a central role in facilitating recovery efforts, coordinating resources, and implementing strategies to enhance resilience and preparedness for future crises."

As she spoke, images of communities coming together to rebuild, volunteers providing assistance to those in need, and infrastructure being restored filled the screen, illustrating the resilience and determination of communities in the face of adversity.

"The first aspect of post-crisis recovery is rebuilding infrastructure and restoring essential services," Dr. Carter continued. "Public administrators must assess damages, prioritize recovery efforts, and mobilize resources to repair critical infrastructure such as roads, bridges, utilities, and communication networks. They must also restore essential services such as healthcare, education, and transportation to support the recovery process and meet the needs of affected communities."

A hand shot up from a student named Marcus. "How do public administrators prioritize recovery efforts, especially when resources are limited and needs are diverse?"

"Public administrators prioritize recovery efforts based on the principle of 'build back better,'" Dr. Carter replied. "They assess damages and prioritize investments in infrastructure and services that enhance resilience, mitigate future risks, and promote sustainable development. They engage with stakeholders, including community members, businesses, and non-governmental organizations, to identify needs, allocate resources, and coordinate recovery efforts effectively."

She clicked to the next slide, which read: "Addressing Social and Economic Impacts."

"The next aspect of post-crisis recovery is addressing the social and economic impacts of the crisis," Dr. Carter explained. "Crises often exacerbate existing social and economic inequalities, disproportionately affecting vulnerable populations such as low-income communities, minorities, and the elderly. Public administrators must implement measures to address these disparities, provide support to affected individuals and families, and promote inclusive and equitable recovery efforts."

A student named Emily raised her hand. "How do public administrators address social and economic disparities in post-crisis recovery efforts?"

"Public administrators address social and economic disparities by implementing targeted interventions and support programs," Dr. Carter replied. "They provide financial assistance, housing support, healthcare services, and mental health resources to affected individuals and families. They also promote economic recovery through job creation programs, small business support initiatives, and investment in local industries and infrastructure. Additionally, they foster social cohesion and community resilience through outreach programs, cultural initiatives, and social services that address the diverse needs of communities."

She clicked to the next slide, which displayed the phrase: "Building Resilience for the Future."

"The final aspect of post-crisis recovery is building resilience for the future," Dr. Carter said. "Resilience is the ability of communities to withstand, adapt to, and recover from crises and disruptions. Public administrators must implement strategies to enhance resilience, such as strengthening infrastructure, improving emergency preparedness and response capabilities, and promoting sustainable development practices that mitigate risks and build adaptive capacity."

As the lecture continued, Dr. Carter guided her students through a detailed exploration of post-crisis recovery and resilience, highlighting the strategies and initiatives employed by public administrators to facilitate recovery, rebuild communities, and enhance resilience in the aftermath of crises. From rebuilding infrastructure and restoring essential services to addressing social and economic impacts and building resilience for the future, these efforts offered valuable insights into the importance of long-term sustainability and preparedness in mitigating the impact of future crises.

"As you reflect on these post-crisis recovery efforts," Dr. Carter concluded, "consider the resilience and determination of communities in overcoming adversity and rebuilding stronger in the aftermath of crises. By embracing recovery as an opportunity for growth and transformation, public administrators can foster resilience, promote sustainability, and build more adaptive and resilient communities prepared to face future challenges."

The students left the lecture hall, their minds buzzing with newfound insights from the captivating exploration of post-crisis recovery and resilience presented by Dr. Carter. Dr. Carter watched them go, knowing that they had gained valuable perspectives on the critical role of public administrators in guiding recovery efforts and building resilience in an increasingly uncertain world.

Case Studies in Crisis Management

Dr. Emily Carter, an esteemed scholar in crisis management, delved into real-world case studies to illustrate the principles and challenges of crisis management. This subpoint offered valuable insights into the application of theoretical knowledge in practical settings, highlighting successful strategies and lessons learned from past crises.

"Let's turn our attention to real-world examples of crisis management," Dr. Carter began, her voice carrying a sense of urgency and purpose. "Through case studies, we can gain valuable insights into the complexities of crisis management and the strategies employed by public administrators to navigate through adversity."

She clicked to the first case study, unveiling the title: "Hurricane Katrina: A Case of Complex Crisis Management."

"Hurricane Katrina was one of the most devastating natural disasters in U.S. history," Dr. Carter explained. "The storm's impact was compounded by failures in disaster preparedness, response, and recovery efforts, leading to widespread devastation and loss of life. Public administrators faced immense challenges in coordinating response efforts, evacuating vulnerable populations, and providing assistance to affected communities."

As she spoke, images of flooded neighborhoods, overwhelmed emergency shelters, and stranded survivors filled the screen, illustrating the magnitude of the crisis and the challenges faced by public administrators in managing the disaster.

"The response to Hurricane Katrina highlighted the importance of effective communication, coordination, and leadership in crisis management," Dr. Carter continued. "While there were notable failures in the response efforts, there were also examples of resilience, resourcefulness, and community solidarity in the face of adversity. Public administrators learned valuable lessons from the crisis, leading to improvements in disaster preparedness, response capabilities, and interagency coordination in subsequent disasters."

A hand shot up from a student named Marcus. "What were some of the key lessons learned from the response to Hurricane Katrina, and how have they influenced crisis management strategies?"

"Key lessons learned from the response to Hurricane Katrina include the importance of effective leadership, coordination, and communication in crisis management," Dr. Carter replied. "Public administrators realized the need for clear command structures, robust communication systems, and coordinated response efforts across all levels of government and with non-governmental organizations and the private sector. Additionally, there was a renewed emphasis on disaster preparedness, community resilience, and equity in emergency response planning and resource allocation."

She clicked to the next case study, which read: "COVID-19 Pandemic: A Global Crisis Response."

"The COVID-19 pandemic has presented unprecedented challenges for public administrators worldwide," Dr. Carter said. "From managing public health crises to addressing economic impacts and social disruptions, public administrators have faced multifaceted challenges in responding to the pandemic. They have implemented a range of strategies, including lockdowns, testing and vaccination campaigns, economic stimulus measures, and public health communication initiatives, to mitigate the spread of the virus and support affected communities."

As she spoke, images of healthcare workers on the frontlines, vaccination centers, and empty streets during lockdowns filled the screen, illustrating the global impact of the pandemic and the diverse response efforts implemented by public administrators.

"The response to the COVID-19 pandemic has underscored the importance of flexibility, adaptability, and innovation in crisis management," Dr. Carter continued. "Public administrators have had to rapidly adjust their strategies and policies in response to evolving scientific evidence, changing public health guidelines, and shifting social and economic conditions. They have leveraged technology, data-driven decision-making, and community partnerships to enhance the effectiveness of response efforts and support resilience and recovery."

As the lecture continued, Dr. Carter guided her students through a detailed exploration of case studies in crisis management, offering valuable insights into the principles, challenges, and strategies employed by public administrators in responding to complex crises. From Hurricane Katrina to the COVID-19 pandemic, these case studies provided a rich tapestry of experiences and lessons learned, highlighting the resilience and resourcefulness of communities and the pivotal role of public administrators in guiding response and recovery efforts in times of crisis.

"As you reflect on these case studies," Dr. Carter concluded, "consider the challenges and opportunities presented by complex crises and the strategies employed by public administrators to navigate through adversity. By learning from past experiences and embracing innovation and collaboration, public administrators can build more resilient and prepared communities capable of facing future challenges with strength and resolve."

The students left the lecture hall, their minds buzzing with newfound insights from the captivating exploration of case studies in crisis management presented by Dr. Carter. Dr. Carter watched them go, knowing that they had gained valuable perspectives on the critical role of public administrators in guiding response and recovery efforts in an increasingly uncertain world.

15

Chapter 15: Future Directions in Public Administration

Emerging Trends in Public Administration

Dr. Emily Carter, a visionary scholar in public administration, embarked on a journey into the future of governance, exploring emerging trends that would shape the landscape of public administration in the years to come. This subpoint illuminated the evolving challenges, opportunities, and innovations that would define the practice of public administration in the 21st century.

"Welcome to the final chapter of our journey," Dr. Carter began, her voice infused with anticipation and excitement. "Today, we peer into the future of public administration, examining emerging trends that will shape the governance landscape in the years ahead."

She clicked to the first slide, unveiling the title: "Emerging Trends in Public Administration."

"The world is evolving at an unprecedented pace,"

Dr. Carter explained. "Technological advancements, demographic shifts, and global challenges are reshaping the way we govern and deliver public services. Public administrators must anticipate and adapt to these changes, embracing innovation, collaboration, and flexibility to address emerging challenges and opportunities."

As she spoke, images of smart cities, artificial intelligence, and global partnerships filled the screen, illustrating the diverse trends and forces shaping the future of public administration.

"The first emerging trend in public administration is the rise of digital governance and e-government initiatives," Dr. Carter continued. "Technological innovations, such as artificial intelligence, blockchain, and big data analytics, are revolutionizing the way governments interact with citizens, deliver services, and make decisions. E-government initiatives are enhancing efficiency, transparency, and citizen engagement, while also posing new challenges related to data privacy, cybersecurity, and digital equity."

A hand shot up from a student named Marcus. "How do you see digital governance transforming the role of public administrators in the future?"

"Digital governance will transform the role of public administrators by enhancing their ability to collect, analyze, and utilize data to inform decision-making, improve service delivery, and address complex challenges," Dr. Carter replied. "Public administrators will need to develop digital literacy skills, embrace data-driven approaches, and foster collaboration across sectors to harness the potential of digital technologies for public good. Additionally, they will need to navigate ethical and regulatory considerations related to data privacy, cybersecurity, and digital inclusion to ensure that digital governance benefits all citizens."

She clicked to the next slide, which read: "Globalization and Interconnected Governance."

"The next emerging trend is the increasing interconnectedness of governance systems and the rise of global challenges that transcend national borders," Dr. Carter explained. "Globalization has transformed the way we govern, requiring public administrators to collaborate across sectors, jurisdictions, and countries to address issues such as climate change, pandemics, and migration. Interconnected governance approaches, such as networked governance and multilateral partnerships, are essential for tackling these complex challenges and promoting sustainable development and peace."

A student named Emily raised her hand. "How can public administrators navigate the complexities of interconnected governance and promote collaboration across diverse stakeholders?"

"Public administrators can navigate the complexities of interconnected governance by fostering trust, communication, and cooperation among diverse stakeholders," Dr. Carter replied. "They can establish collaborative platforms, such as intergovernmental organizations, public-private partnerships, and civil society forums, to facilitate dialogue, share resources, and coordinate action on shared challenges. Additionally, they can leverage technology and data-sharing mechanisms to enhance transparency, accountability, and mutual understanding among stakeholders. By promoting inclusive and participatory approaches to governance, public administrators can build resilient and adaptive systems capable of addressing global challenges in a coordinated and effective manner."

She clicked to the next slide, which displayed the phrase: "Innovative Service Delivery Models."

"The final emerging trend is the emergence of innovative service delivery models that prioritize citizen-centered approaches, outcomes-based accountability, and cross-sector collaboration," Dr. Carter said. "Public administrators are exploring new ways to deliver services that are responsive to the diverse needs and preferences of citizens, leverage technology and data to improve efficiency and effectiveness, and engage with non-governmental actors to co-create solutions and maximize impact. From collaborative governance initiatives to social innovation hubs, these innovative models are transforming the way we govern and deliver public services in the 21st century."

As the lecture continued, Dr. Carter guided her students through a detailed exploration of emerging trends in public administration, offering valuable insights into the challenges, opportunities, and innovations that would shape the future of governance. From digital governance and globalization to innovative service delivery models, these trends provided a glimpse into the evolving landscape of public administration and the transformative potential of proactive and forward-thinking leadership.

"As you reflect on these emerging trends," Dr. Carter concluded, "consider the opportunities and challenges they present for public administrators and the strategies needed to navigate through uncertainty and complexity. By embracing innovation, collaboration, and adaptability, public administrators can shape a more inclusive, resilient, and sustainable future for governance and public service delivery."

The students left the lecture hall, their minds buzzing

with excitement and anticipation for the future of public administration presented by Dr. Carter. Dr. Carter watched them go, knowing that they had gained valuable perspectives on the critical role of proactive and forward-thinking leadership in shaping the governance landscape in an increasingly interconnected and dynamic world.

Role of Technology in Shaping Future Governance

Dr. Emily Carter, an innovative thinker in public administration, delved into the transformative role of technology in shaping the future of governance. This subpoint explored the opportunities and challenges presented by technological advancements, highlighting the potential for digital innovation to revolutionize the way governments operate and deliver public services.

"Let's explore the profound impact of technology on the future of governance," Dr. Carter began, her voice brimming with enthusiasm. "As we enter an era of unprecedented technological advancement, we are witnessing a fundamental shift in the way governments interact with citizens, manage resources, and address societal challenges."

She clicked to the first slide, unveiling the title: "Role of Technology in Shaping Future Governance."

"The rapid evolution of technology is reshaping the landscape of governance," Dr. Carter explained. "From artificial intelligence and automation to blockchain and the Internet of Things, technological innovations are revolutionizing the way governments operate, enabling them to deliver services more efficiently, transparently, and responsively. Technology has the potential to enhance citizen engagement, improve decision-making, and promote innovation across all aspects of governance."

As she spoke, images of smart cities, digital platforms, and innovative government services filled the screen, illustrating the transformative potential of technology in reshaping the future of governance.

"The first aspect of technology's role in shaping future governance is the use of data and analytics to inform decision-making and improve service delivery," Dr. Carter continued. "Governments are increasingly leveraging data-driven approaches to gain insights into citizen needs, preferences, and behaviors, allowing them to tailor services, allocate resources, and prioritize initiatives more effectively. From predictive analytics to performance dashboards, data-driven governance enables governments to make informed decisions and measure outcomes in real-time, enhancing accountability and transparency."

A hand shot up from a student named Marcus. "How can governments ensure the ethical use of data and analytics in decision-making?"

"Governments can ensure the ethical use of data and analytics by establishing clear guidelines, regulations, and safeguards to protect privacy, security, and civil liberties," Dr. Carter replied. "They can implement robust data governance frameworks that define data ownership, access rights, and usage policies, ensuring that data is collected, stored, and analyzed responsibly and ethically. Additionally, governments can promote transparency and accountability by involving citizens in the decision-making process, providing access to data and information, and soliciting feedback and oversight from independent bodies and experts."

She clicked to the next slide, which read: "Digital Transformation of Government Services."

"The next aspect of technology's role in shaping future governance is the digital transformation of government services," Dr. Carter explained. "Governments are embracing digital platforms, mobile applications, and online portals to deliver services more efficiently, conveniently, and inclusively. Digital government services enable citizens to access information, apply for benefits, and interact with government agencies anytime, anywhere, and on any device, reducing bureaucracy, enhancing accessibility, and improving the overall citizen experience."

A student named Emily raised her hand. "How can governments ensure that digital government services are accessible and inclusive for all citizens, including those with limited digital literacy or access to technology?"

"Governments can ensure that digital government services are accessible and inclusive by adopting a user-centered design approach and providing multiple channels for access and support," Dr. Carter replied. "They can design digital platforms and applications that are intuitive, user-friendly, and compatible with a range of devices and assistive technologies. Additionally, they can offer in-person assistance, telephone hotlines, and community outreach programs to help citizens navigate digital services and address barriers to access. By prioritizing accessibility and inclusivity, governments can ensure that all citizens can benefit from the convenience and efficiency of digital government services."

As the lecture continued, Dr. Carter guided her students through a detailed exploration of the role of technology in shaping future governance, offering valuable insights into the opportunities and challenges presented by digital innovation. From data-driven decision-making to the digital transformation of government services, technology's transformative potential provided a glimpse into the future of governance and public service delivery in an increasingly digital and interconnected world.

"As you reflect on the role of technology in shaping future governance," Dr. Carter concluded, "consider the opportunities and challenges it presents for governments and the strategies needed to harness its transformative potential for public good. By embracing innovation, collaboration, and citizen-centric approaches, governments can build more responsive, inclusive, and effective systems of governance capable of addressing the complex challenges of the 21st century."

The students left the lecture hall, their minds buzzing with excitement and anticipation for the transformative potential of technology in shaping the future of governance presented by Dr. Carter. Dr. Carter watched them go, knowing that they had gained valuable perspectives on the critical role of digital innovation in shaping the future of public administration in an increasingly digital and interconnected world.

Innovation and Change Management

Dr. Emily Carter, a visionary leader in public administration, embarked on a journey into the realm of innovation and change management, exploring the strategies and practices needed to foster innovation and navigate organizational change in the public sector. This subpoint illuminated the transformative potential of innovation and the challenges inherent in managing change in bureaucratic environments.

"Let's delve into the dynamic world of innovation and change management," Dr. Carter began, her voice resonating with energy and determination. "Innovation is the lifeblood of progress, and change is the catalyst for transformation. In today's rapidly evolving world, public administrators must embrace innovation and adapt to change to thrive in an increasingly complex and interconnected environment."

She clicked to the first slide, unveiling the title: "Innovation and Change Management."

"Innovation is not just about new technologies or flashy ideas," Dr. Carter explained. "It's about challenging the status quo, fostering creativity, and embracing continuous improvement to drive meaningful change and deliver better outcomes for citizens. Change management is the process of guiding individuals, teams, and organizations through transitions, overcoming resistance, and building capacity for innovation and adaptation."

As she spoke, images of innovative projects, collaborative workshops, and transformational leaders filled the screen, illustrating the dynamic nature of innovation and change management in the public sector.

"The first aspect of innovation and change management is creating a culture of innovation within organizations," Dr. Carter continued. "Organizational culture plays a critical role in shaping attitudes, behaviors, and practices related to innovation. Leaders must cultivate an environment that values experimentation, learning, and risk-taking, where employees feel empowered to challenge conventions, explore new ideas, and collaborate across silos."

A hand shot up from a student named Marcus. "How can

public administrators foster a culture of innovation within bureaucratic organizations?"

"Public administrators can foster a culture of innovation by leading by example, promoting open communication, and incentivizing creativity and collaboration," Dr. Carter replied. "They can create opportunities for employees to participate in innovation initiatives, such as hackathons, design thinking workshops, and innovation labs, where they can generate ideas, prototype solutions, and test new approaches in a safe and supportive environment. Additionally, they can recognize and reward innovative efforts, celebrate successes, and learn from failures to cultivate a culture of continuous improvement and learning."

She clicked to the next slide, which read: "Strategies for Navigating Organizational Change."

"The next aspect of innovation and change management is navigating organizational change," Dr. Carter explained. "Change is inevitable in today's fast-paced world, but it can also be challenging, especially in bureaucratic environments where processes, structures, and cultures are deeply entrenched. Public administrators must employ effective change management strategies to overcome resistance, build buy-in, and sustain momentum for innovation and transformation."

A student named Emily raised her hand. "What are some effective change management strategies for public administrators?"

"Effective change management strategies for public administrators include communicating a compelling vision for change, engaging stakeholders early and often, and building capacity for change through training, coaching, and support," Dr. Carter replied. "They can create change management teams or task forces to lead change efforts, establish clear goals, timelines, and metrics for success, and monitor progress and adjust strategies as needed. Additionally, they can foster a culture of resilience and adaptability, encouraging flexibility, agility, and continuous learning to navigate uncertainty and complexity."

As the lecture continued, Dr. Carter guided her students through a detailed exploration of innovation and change management, offering valuable insights into the strategies and practices needed to foster innovation and navigate organizational change in the public sector. From creating a culture of innovation to navigating complex transitions, innovation and change management provided a roadmap for public administrators to drive meaningful change and deliver better outcomes for citizens in an increasingly dynamic and uncertain world.

"As you reflect on the principles of innovation and change management," Dr. Carter concluded, "consider the opportunities and challenges they present for public administrators and the strategies needed to foster a culture of innovation and navigate organizational change. By embracing innovation and leading with vision and purpose, public administrators can build more responsive, resilient, and effective organizations capable of addressing the complex challenges of the 21st century."

The students left the lecture hall, their minds buzzing with excitement and inspiration from the captivating exploration of innovation and change management presented by Dr. Carter. Dr. Carter watched them go, knowing that they had gained valuable perspectives on the critical role of innovation and change management in shaping the future of public administration in an increasingly dynamic and interconnected world.

Sustainability and Environmental Governance

Dr. Emily Carter, a passionate advocate for sustainability and environmental governance, embarked on a journey into the realm of environmental stewardship and sustainable development. This subpoint illuminated the critical importance of integrating environmental considerations into public administration practices and policies to address pressing environmental challenges and promote long-term sustainability.

"Let us delve into the vital realm of sustainability and environmental governance," Dr. Carter began, her voice resonating with urgency and conviction. "In today's world, the imperative of sustainability has never been clearer. As stewards of the public interest, it is incumbent upon us, as public administrators, to prioritize environmental considerations in our decision-making processes and policies."

She clicked to the first slide, unveiling the title: "Sustainability and Environmental Governance."

"Sustainability is not merely a buzzword; it is a guiding principle that encompasses the need to balance economic prosperity, social equity, and environmental protection," Dr. Carter explained. "Environmental governance refers to the mechanisms, processes, and institutions through which environmental policies are formulated, implemented, and evaluated. It involves collaboration among governments, businesses, civil society, and other stakeholders to address environmental challenges and promote sustainable development."

As she spoke, images of pristine landscapes, renewable energy projects, and sustainable cities filled the screen, illustrating the interconnectedness of human society and the natural world, and the importance of environmental governance in safeguarding our planet's future.

"The first aspect of sustainability and environmental governance is recognizing the interconnectedness of environmental, social, and economic systems," Dr. Carter continued. "Environmental degradation, climate change, and biodiversity loss pose existential threats to human well-being and planetary health. Public administrators must adopt a holistic approach to governance that integrates environmental considerations into decision-making processes and policies, promotes sustainable practices, and fosters resilience to environmental risks and disruptions."

A hand shot up from a student named Marcus. "How can public administrators promote sustainability and environmental governance in their organizations and communities?"

"Public administrators can promote sustainability and environmental governance by setting ambitious sustainability goals, developing comprehensive sustainability plans, and implementing strategies to reduce carbon emissions, conserve natural resources, and protect ecosystems," Dr. Carter replied. "They can integrate environmental considerations into procurement policies, land-use planning, and infrastructure development, prioritize investments in clean energy, public transportation, and green infrastructure, and engage with stakeholders to raise awareness, mobilize support, and foster collaboration for sustainable development. By leading by example and partnering with others, public administrators can catalyze positive change and build a more sustainable and resilient future for all."

She clicked to the next slide, which read: "Addressing Climate Change and Promoting Resilience."

"The next aspect of sustainability and environmental governance is addressing climate change and promoting resilience," Dr. Carter explained. "Climate change is one of the most pressing challenges of our time, with far-reaching implications for ecosystems, economies, and societies. Public administrators must take urgent action to mitigate greenhouse gas emissions, adapt to changing climate conditions, and build resilience to climate-related risks and disasters. This requires innovative policies, investments, and partnerships at all levels of government and society."

A student named Emily raised her hand. "How can public administrators effectively address climate change and promote resilience in their communities?"

"Public administrators can effectively address climate change and promote resilience by implementing climate action plans, setting emission reduction targets, and investing in renewable energy, energy efficiency, and climate-resilient infrastructure," Dr. Carter replied. "They can integrate climate considerations into land-use planning, transportation, and disaster risk management, mainstream climate adaptation and resilience into decision-making processes and policies, and engage with communities to build awareness, capacity, and support for climate action. By adopting a proactive and collaborative approach, public administrators can help communities adapt to the impacts of climate change and build a more sustainable and resilient future for all."

As the lecture continued, Dr. Carter guided her students through a detailed exploration of sustainability and environmental governance, offering valuable insights into the critical importance of integrating environmental considerations into public administration practices and policies. From recognizing the interconnectedness of environmental, social, and economic systems to addressing climate change and promoting resilience, sustainability and environmental governance provided a roadmap for public administrators to build a more sustainable and resilient future for all.

"As you reflect on the principles of sustainability and environmental governance," Dr. Carter concluded, "consider the opportunities and challenges they present for public administrators and the strategies needed to integrate environmental considerations into decision-making processes and policies. By embracing sustainability and environmental stewardship, public administrators can contribute to a healthier, more prosperous, and more sustainable future for current and future generations."

The students left the lecture hall, their minds buzzing with inspiration and determination from the captivating exploration of sustainability and environmental governance presented by Dr. Carter. Dr. Carter watched them go, knowing that they had gained valuable perspectives on the critical importance of integrating environmental considerations into public administration practices and policies to address pressing environmental challenges and promote long-term sustainability.

Global Challenges and Public Administration

Dr. Emily Carter, an esteemed scholar in public administration, embarked on an exploration of the profound impact of global challenges on the practice of public administration. This subpoint illuminated the interconnected nature of contemporary global issues and the imperative for public administrators to respond effectively to complex, transnational challenges.

"Let us now turn our attention to the pressing global challenges facing public administration," Dr. Carter began, her voice echoing with gravitas and purpose. "In an increasingly interconnected world, the challenges we face transcend national borders and require collaborative, innovative solutions that transcend traditional bureaucratic boundaries."

She clicked to the first slide, unveiling the title: "Global Challenges and Public Administration."

"As public administrators, we cannot afford to ignore the interconnected nature of contemporary global issues," Dr. Carter explained. "From climate change and pandemics to terrorism and refugee crises, the challenges we face are multifaceted, dynamic, and interrelated. They demand coordinated action, strategic foresight, and adaptive governance approaches that transcend siloed thinking and embrace complexity."

As she spoke, images of melting ice caps, crowded refugee camps, and global health crises filled the screen, illustrating the urgency and complexity of the global challenges facing public administration in the 21st century.

"The first aspect of global challenges and public administration is recognizing the interconnectedness of contemporary issues," Dr. Carter continued. "Climate change, for example, affects not only the environment but also economies, societies, and geopolitics. Similarly, pandemics like COVID-19 have profound implications for public health, economies, and governance systems worldwide. Public administrators must adopt a holistic approach to governance that acknowledges the interconnected nature of global challenges and seeks integrated, collaborative solutions that address root causes and systemic vulnerabilities."

A hand shot up from a student named Marcus. "How can public administrators effectively respond to complex, transnational challenges like climate change and pandemics?"

"Public administrators can effectively respond to complex, transnational challenges by fostering international cooperation, leveraging multilateral partnerships, and promoting evidence-based policymaking," Dr. Carter replied. "They can engage with international organizations, civil society, and the private sector to share knowledge, resources, and best practices, coordinate responses, and build capacity for prevention, mitigation, and adaptation. Additionally, they can invest in scientific research, data analytics, and early warning systems to better understand and anticipate emerging risks and inform decision-making at all levels of government and society."

She clicked to the next slide, which read: "Promoting Global Governance and Diplomacy."

"The next aspect of global challenges and public administration is promoting global governance and diplomacy," Dr. Carter explained. "In an interconnected world, effective governance requires collaboration, diplomacy, and dialogue among nations, regions, and stakeholders. Public administrators play a critical role in shaping international agendas, negotiating agreements, and implementing commitments that address shared challenges and promote collective action for the common good."

A student named Emily raised her hand. "How can public administrators navigate the complexities of global governance and diplomacy in an increasingly polarized and uncertain world?"

"Public administrators can navigate the complexities of global governance and diplomacy by building trust, fostering dialogue, and promoting inclusivity and equity in decision-making processes," Dr. Carter replied. "They can engage with diverse stakeholders, including marginalized communities, indigenous peoples, and youth, to ensure that their voices are heard and their perspectives are integrated into policy discussions and negotiations. Additionally, they can promote transparency, accountability, and respect for human rights in all aspects of governance, strengthening the legitimacy and effectiveness of global governance institutions and processes."

As the lecture continued, Dr. Carter guided her students through a detailed exploration of the profound impact of global challenges on the practice of public administration, offering valuable insights into the imperative for collaborative, innovative solutions to address complex, transnational issues. From recognizing the interconnectedness of contemporary issues to promoting global governance and diplomacy, global challenges and public administration provided a roadmap for public administrators to navigate the complexities of an interconnected world and build a more resilient, equitable, and sustainable future for all.

"As you reflect on the implications of global challenges for public administration," Dr. Carter concluded, "consider the opportunities and challenges they present for governance and the strategies needed to foster international cooperation, build resilience, and promote collective action for the common good. By embracing complexity and collaboration, public administrators can play a vital role in addressing the urgent global challenges of the 21st century and building a more just, peaceful, and sustainable world."

The students left the lecture hall, their minds buzzing with inspiration and determination from the captivating exploration of global challenges and public administration presented by Dr. Carter. Dr. Carter watched them go, knowing that they had gained valuable perspectives on the imperative for collaborative, innovative solutions to address complex, transnational issues in an increasingly interconnected world.

Vision for the Future of Public Administration

Dr. Emily Carter, a visionary leader in public administration, concluded her exploration of the future of public administration with a compelling vision for the years ahead. This final subpoint illuminated the transformative potential of innovative approaches, collaborative governance, and ethical leadership in shaping the future of public administration for the betterment of society.

"As we conclude our journey into the future of public administration, let us dare to envision a future that is bold, inclusive, and equitable," Dr. Carter began, her voice filled with hope and conviction. "The challenges we face are immense, but so too are the opportunities to create positive change and build a more resilient, just, and sustainable world for all."

She clicked to the first slide, unveiling the title: "Vision for the Future of Public Administration."

"Our vision for the future of public administration is one of transformative change, driven by innovation, collaboration, and ethical leadership," Dr. Carter explained. "It is a future where public administrators embrace complexity, uncertainty, and diversity as opportunities for learning, adaptation, and growth. It is a future where governance is participatory, transparent, and accountable, where decisions are informed by evidence, science, and the voices of all stakeholders. It is a future where public service is valued, respected, and inclusive, where diversity is celebrated, and where public servants are empowered to make a difference in the lives of others."

As she spoke, images of diverse communities, vibrant cities, and sustainable landscapes filled the screen, illustrating the aspirational vision of a future where public administration serves as a force for positive change and social progress.

"The first aspect of our vision for the future of public administration is embracing innovation and technology to enhance service delivery, improve efficiency, and promote inclusivity," Dr. Carter continued. "Innovative technologies such as artificial intelligence, blockchain, and big data analytics hold immense potential to revolutionize governance, empower citizens, and address complex challenges such as climate change, inequality, and public health. Public administrators must harness the power of technology to foster innovation, creativity, and collaboration across sectors and borders, and to build a more responsive, resilient, and equitable public administration for the 21st century."

A hand shot up from a student named Marcus. "What role do you see for ethical leadership in shaping the future of public administration?"

"Ethical leadership is the cornerstone of effective governance and public service," Dr. Carter replied. "In an era of increasing complexity, uncertainty, and disruption, ethical leadership is essential to build trust, inspire confidence, and navigate ethical dilemmas with integrity and accountability. Public administrators must uphold high ethical standards, promote transparency, honesty, and fairness, and act in the public interest at all times. They must prioritize the well-being of society and future generations over short-term gains or personal interests, and champion values such as justice, equity, and human rights in all aspects of governance and decision-making."

She clicked to the next slide, which read: "Fostering Collaboration and Partnerships."

"The next aspect of our vision for the future of public administration is fostering collaboration and partnerships," Dr. Carter explained. "In an interconnected world, complex challenges require collective action and collaborative solutions that transcend traditional boundaries and silos. Public administrators must forge partnerships with governments, civil society, academia, and the private sector to mobilize resources, share knowledge, and coordinate responses to shared challenges. By working together across sectors and disciplines, we can leverage our collective expertise, resources, and influence to address the urgent issues facing our planet and build a more sustainable and resilient future for all."

As the lecture concluded, Dr. Carter left her students with a sense of hope and determination, urging them to embrace the transformative potential of innovative approaches, collaborative governance, and ethical leadership in shaping the future of public administration. From embracing innovation and technology to fostering collaboration and partnerships, the vision for the future of public administration provided a roadmap for public administrators to navigate the complexities of an uncertain world and build a more just, inclusive, and sustainable future for all.

"As you reflect on our vision for the future of public administration," Dr. Carter concluded, "consider the opportunities and challenges it presents for governance and the strategies needed to turn this vision into reality. By embracing innovation, collaboration, and ethical leadership, public administrators can play a vital role in building a more resilient, equitable, and sustainable future for current and future generations."

The students left the lecture hall, their minds buzzing with inspiration and determination from the captivating vision for the future of public administration presented by Dr. Carter. Dr. Carter watched them go, knowing that they had gained valuable perspectives on the transformative potential of innovative approaches, collaborative governance, and ethical leadership in shaping the future of public administration for the betterment of society.

About the Author

Goodson Mumba is a multifaceted individual known for his diverse expertise and prolific contributions across various fields. As an infopreneur, thought leader, and spiritual leader, he has inspired countless individuals through his insightful teachings and impactful writings. Mumba is also an accomplished author, with several notable works to his name, including "Understanding Corporate Worship," "The Years I Spent in a Week," "Management By Harmony," "The CEO's Diary," "Change to Change" and "Creative Thinking for results" His literary works span topics ranging from business management to personal development and spirituality, reflecting his broad range of interests and insights.

With a Master of Business Leadership (MBL) and a Bachelor of Arts in Theology (BTh), Mumba brings a unique blend of business acumen and spiritual wisdom to his work. His educational background is further enriched by a Group Diploma in Management Studies, providing him with a solid foundation in organizational dynamics and leadership principles. Additionally, Mumba holds diplomas in Education

Psychology, Leadership and Management Styles, Organizational Behaviour, Financial Accounting, Economic Growth and Development, and Project Management, showcasing his commitment to continuous learning and professional development.

Mumba's expertise extends beyond traditional academic disciplines, encompassing areas such as Neuro-Linguistic Programming (NLP) and Positive Psychology. His diverse skill set is complemented by a range of certifications, including Creative Problem Solving and Decision Making, Life Coaching Fundamentals and Techniques, Professional Life Coaching, and Performance Management System Design. These certifications reflect Mumba's dedication to equipping himself with the tools and knowledge necessary to empower others and drive positive change.

As an author, Mumba's writings reflect his deep understanding of human nature, organizational dynamics, and spiritual principles. His works offer practical insights, actionable strategies, and inspirational guidance for individuals seeking personal growth, professional success, and spiritual fulfillment. Mumba's holistic approach to life and leadership resonates with readers worldwide, making him a respected figure in both the business and spiritual communities.

Overall, Goodson Mumba's diverse background, extensive knowledge, and profound insights make him a sought-after speaker, mentor, and author. His commitment to excellence, lifelong learning, and service to others continues to inspire individuals to unlock their full potential and lead lives of purpose and significance.

Goodson Mumba is renowned for initiating the concept of Management by Harmony, revolutionizing traditional management practices with a focus on balanced and holistic approaches. He has authored two influential books on this subject: "Introduction to Management by Harmony" and its sequel, "Management by Harmony."

Mumba's work has significantly impacted the field, offering innovative strategies for fostering organizational harmony and efficiency. His contributions continue to shape contemporary management theories and practices.